W9-AQC-905

Saint Francis of Assisi

TWAS 409

St. Francis of Assisi

SAINT FRANCIS OF ASSISI

By LAWRENCE S. CUNNINGHAM
The Florida State University

TWAYNE PUBLISHERS

A DIVISION OF G. K. HALL & CO., BOSTON

Library of Congress Cataloging in Publication Data

Cunningham, Lawrence.
  Saint Francis of Assisi.

  (Twayne's world authors series ; TWAS 409)
  Bibliography: p. 143 - 47.
  Includes index.
  1. Francesco d'Assisi, Saint, 1182-1226.
BX4700.F6C785
ISBN 0-8057-6249-3   271'.3'024 [B]   76-14216

Contents

About the Author

Preface

Chronology

1. The Prose Writings of Saint Francis of Assisi   13

2. The Prayers and the Poetry   42

3. The *Legendae* of Saint Francis   77

4. The Franciscan Revival of Modern Times   109

Notes and References   131

Selected Bibliography   143

Index   149

About the Author

Lawrence S. Cunningham has a Licentiate in Theology *cum laude* from the Gregorian University in Rome and MA in English Literature and the Ph.D. in Humanities (with an emphasis in religion and literature) from Florida State University. He is associate professor of Religion at Florida State and has also served (for three years) as associate director of the Florida State University Study Center in Florence, Italy.

Dr. Cunningham's first book *Brother Francis* (Harper and Row, 1972) was also on Saint Francis and he is currently working on a translation of Bonaventure's *Itinerarium Mentis ad Deum* for Abbey Press. He has published over thirty articles on various aspects of religion and culture. His long range project is a study of religious autobiography of convert Catholics from Newman to the present.

Preface

When Goethe visited Assisi in the late eighteenth century the only thing that he thought worthy of his attention was the Roman temple that looks out over the main square of the city. After admiring the edifice he left the city in some haste; Goethe showed no desire to see the Romanesque Basilica of Saint Francis or the paintings of Giotto, Cimabue, and Lorenzetti; nor did he evince the slightest curiosity about the man who inspired that outpouring of art: Francesco Bernardone, better known to the world as Saint Francis of Assisi. It was left to the nineteenth century savants, critics, and scholars such as Jules Michelet, Matthew Arnold, and, above all, Paul Sabatier to rescue Saint Francis of Assisi from the relative obscurity in which he had fallen outside of Catholic circles since the time of the Renaissance.

In a sense, we today are still living with the nineteenth century Romantic rediscovery of Saint Francis of Assisi. In the popular imagination Francis is the harmless but charming nature mystic, the lover of animals, and the divine troubadour. He was considered the source and inspiration of those painters of the Trecento and Quattrocento who breathed nature and humanity into the static art of the Italo-Byzantine period. He was singled out as the person who stood in open contradiction to the statically hieratic church of Pope Innocent III. This romantic picture of Francis has its final flowering today in the innumerable bad cement statues that one can buy in garden shops depicting the saint with a bird on his shoulders, suitable for garden or pond: Saint Francis of Assisi as a medieval Doctor Doolitle or, with more sophistication, the patron saint of ecology.

A closer look at Saint Francis in the context of his own time — and scholars have been taking such looks for nearly a century — not only reveals a far more complex person but one who has had an immense impact on medieval spirituality, the development of political theory, the history of art, and the emergence of Italian literature.

Only in more recent times has much attention been paid to Saint Francis as a writer. To be sure, there has been a continued admiration for the *Canticle of Brother Sun* (Matthew Arnold translated and commented on it) but the bulk of his prose writings and his prayers were strictly the province of the pious and the scholarly. The last generation of scholars has shown much more eagerness to reexamine and study his writings as a source of information for the reconstruction of his life and his ideals. This has been a shift from an intense study of the legends and biographies that sprung up after his death (1226) in order to study Francis from the vantage of what he wrote. It is now generally recognized that the writings have an immense importance for the study of Francis and the whole movement of Franciscanism.

This book, then, concentrates on Saint Francis the writer. It does not intend to be a work of original scholarship. This book intends to outline for the interested reader what Francis wrote, what significance these writings had, what the current scholarly opinion is about these works, and how they related to the emergence of that spirit in Italy which has been called the "proto-Renaissance," i.e., the epoch prior to the great fifteenth century flowering of the Renaissance. The orientation of this study will be to concentrate more on the cultural influence of these writings and less on the theological influence although, at times, it is difficult to disengage these two strands.

There is a problem in doing a book on Francis as a writer. Some of what he wrote can make little claim to literary merit while other works can make such a claim. But more importantly, his imaginative and poetic genius, the source of much of the literary and artistic influence on others, has been preserved not in his own writings but in the memories of those who followed him. In order to talk of Francis, his ideas, and his poetry one must discuss those memoirs; otherwise, the picture of Francis and his ideas becomes distorted. There are many historical parallels to this situation. One cannot speak of the philosophy of Socrates without reference to the *Dialogues* of Plato just as one cannot talk intelligently about the teachings of Jesus without reference to the Gospels. Naturally there is the great critical problem of disentangling the thought of Francis from the sometimes uncritical adulation of the hagiographer. It is the same problem that one encounters with the "historical" Socrates or Jesus.

This book is divided into three main parts. The first chapter will include a discussion of the prose writings of Francis. It will describe those writings that can be safely ascribed to his pen and their value will be shown both for Franciscan studies and for the larger culture. Of necessity, this will be the least exciting material since these writings tend to be legalistic, flatly written, without literary pretension or elegance. The importance of this material is considerable and, despite their literary lack, these writings deserve close attention for other than literary reasons.

The second chapter is a study of the prayers that Francis composed both for private and liturgical use. These prayers reveal far more of his poetic gifts than do the prose writings. The most important work discussed in this chapter is the *Canticle of Brother Sun*. Its sources will be analyzed, its translation difficulties noted, and its significance will be studied in some detail. The chapter concludes with a description of the tradition of the *lauda* in Italian literature as it was given impetus from the *Canticle* and found its culmination in the poetry of Jacopone da Todi.

The final section of the book treats the biographies and legends (meant literally as those lives of Saint Francis which could be read aloud at liturgical services) that began to appear almost immediately after the death of the saint. It will be shown that the body of literature that begins with the *Sacrum Commercium* and the early lives of Thomas of Celano and continues well into the next century not only had a great influence and a direct impact on artists such as Dante and Giotto but also contained much authentic material about the life and the ideals of the saint himself.

This book concludes with an epilogue to deal with the renewed interest in Francis that began in the last century and continued down into this century having an influence on persons as diverse as the French mystic Simone Weil and the novelists Herman Hesse and Nikos Kazantzakis.

The first draft of this book was written while I served as temporary director of the Florida State University Study Center in Florence, Italy. This opportunity not only provided me with a modicum of leisure to read and write but made it possible to go to those places in Umbria and Tuscany which still breathe the presence of *il Poverello*. The towns of Assisi, Perugia, Gubbio, and the sanctuary of La Verna not only give a sense of the *genius loci* but a feel for the *splendor personae*. I must thank John J. Carey, chairman of the Religion Department at Florida State, for giving me the time to go to

Florence. The permanent director of the Florence Center, Professor Fred Licht, was not only a great help to me but a friend and an inspiration for my work. My debt to him is beyond recounting. My research was also facilitated by the use of the library of the *Kunsthistorisches Institut* in Florence and the Berenson Library of *I Tatti* at Settignano. Finally, my wife Cecilia not only was tolerant of the weekends that we stayed in Florence when I wrote while the Tuscan hills beckoned but shared with me her not inconsiderable knowledge of Italian art and architecture.

English versions of the writings of Saint Francis and from the legends are from the *English Omnibus of the Sources for the Life of Saint Francis* (Chicago, 1973) quoted with permission of the Franciscan Herald Press unless otherwise noted in the footnotes. The quotations from the Holy Scriptures are my own translations from the Latin Vulgate. All other citations from other languages are in my translation unless otherwise noted in the footnotes.

Chronology

(Disputed dates are marked by a second date in parentheses and a question mark.)

1181   Born in Assisi, the child of Pietro and Pica Bernardone.
(1182 ?) Baptized Giovanni, but later renamed Francesco by his father, a moderately well-to-do cloth merchant.

1202   War breaks out between Assisi and Perugia. Francis participates on the side of Assisi, is made prisoner of war of Perugia. Ransomed by father after year's imprisonment.

1204   A year of illness and convalescence.

1205   Beginning of the conversion of Francis and of his alienation from his father. While praying in the abandoned church of San Damiano near Assisi he "hears" the curcifix speak to him.

1206   Francis brought before the bishop of Assisi by his father. After break with his father, goes to Gubbio to minister to lepers. Returning to Assisi, takes up residence at San Damiano, living the life of hermit.

1206 - 08 At San Damiano, praying and restoring the church.

1208   On February 24, 1208, while at Mass hears the passages in Matthew about the life of poverty; determines to follow such a life. First companions join Francis this year. They travel through central Italy on a preaching mission.

1209   Francis and his followers visit Rome and receive approval
(1201 ?) for their rule of life from Pope Innocent III. Later they dwell at the *Portiuncula* (the "Little Portion") of the church of Saint Mary of the Angels in the valley below Assisi.

1211   Francis makes missionary journey to Dalmatia.

1212   Clare of Assisi is received by Francis and initiated into the Franciscan way of life. She and her sisters take up conventual life at San Damiano.

1213 - 15 Period of travel for Francis. Goes to Spain in attempt to reach the Moslem world. Is in Rome during the celebration of the Fourth Lateran Council.

1217 The Pentecost Chapter at Assisi (so-called "chapter of the mats"). Francis proposes to leave again for the Moslem world but is dissuaded.

1219 Francis leaves for the Near East. Visits Acre and Dalmietta. Visits Sultan at Dalmietta after crossing both the Crusader and the Moslem lines.

1220 Returns to Italy. Resigns as head of the Franciscan Order, replaced by Peter Catani.

1221 Writes a new Rule for the Franciscans (so-called *Regula Non-Bullata*). Brother Elias of Cortona the new head of the order.

1222 Francis on preaching tour of Southern Italy.

1223 Rewrites the *Rule of 1221*. Revision debated and accepted at the Pentecost Chapter; finaly approved by Pope Honorius III on November 29. Spends Christmas at Greccio where he has a crib scene set up for the midnight Mass.

1224 Experiences the stigmata while praying on Mount La Verna on September 14 (?).

1225 Francis again on a preaching tour. Crude attempts made to treat his eye illness (contracted in the Middle East?). Writes the *Canticle of Brother Sun* in Assisi during May(?).

1226 After six months of travel, returns to Assisi in broken health. Quartered in the bishop's palace, he adds final verses to the *Canticle*. Dies on October 4 and is buried in the parish church of San Giorgio in Assisi.

1228 Canonized in ceremonies at Assisi by Pope Gregory IX (who was Cardinal Hugolin, his personal friend and a former Cardinal-protector of the Franciscan Order). Body of Saint Francis removed from San Giorgio and reburied in the basilica being built to honor him.

CHAPTER 1

The Prose Writings of
Saint Francis of Assisi

AS the reader will soon learn in some detail, it is almost impossible to pinpoint when Saint Francis of Assisi wrote the works attributed to him. Scholars are forced time and again to fall back on such imprecise evasions as "after 1220" or "in the last years (or months) of his life." Nor is it always clear that he himself actually wrote what is attributed to his pen. We do possess some autographs of his writings (two, to be precise) thus rendering academic the question of whether he could, in fact, write at all. There is also good evidence that at least some of his writings were actually dictated to others who served as his secretaries. Thomas of Celano, his first biographer, says, to cite one example, that early in his career he wrote *(scripsit)* a short rule for his followers whereas Saint Francis, more accurately, says in his *Testament* that he had this rule written down *(feci scribi)*.

The writings of Francis that have survived (there are others we know of that have been lost) were, with the exception of a few of the prayers and the *Canticle of Brother Sun,* written in response to various needs: jurisprudence for his religious order; his last wishes written during the time of his terminal illness; letters written either to be circulated as exhortations or sermons; other letters written in response to specific queries, etc.

It comes then as a bit of a shock to the average reader to discover that Francis of Assisi, a man whose life was one of consummate poetry and who wrote one of the first vernacular poems in Italian, could write such flat and turgid prose on topics that seem no more interesting than medieval Summas or sermons. The language that he most often used was Latin and it was not very polished Latin at that. Indeed, the style of Francis is such that in the analysis of his writings there is a critical rule of thumb to be followed: where an elegant turn of phrase is found or the style shows polish, one always suspects the hand of an editor or a secretary who has finished off the piece.

What schooling Francis did possess came from the rudimentary education that he received from the parish priests of Assisi (probably those who were at the church of San Giorgio, his parish) supplemented by what he learned from the mercantile dealings of his father and by his own native wit. He never attended the university and while he professed a respect for theologians and scholars, there was also a strong distrust of learning and scholarship in him. His writings do show a good familiarity with Sacred Scripture and he quoted the Bible with generous frequency. He also made scattered allusions to some of the Fathers and references to popular proverbs. Beyond that, it is not possible to detect much literary and/or theological influences in his writings. That he knew Latin is evidenced in his prose which is written in that language; his *Canticle* is written in dialectical Italian, and the early biographies tell us that he knew French and that he would often sing in that language.

Apart from the *Canticle* and a few of the prayers, there is little of literary merit in his writings; they are, stylistically, banal and flat. They are, nonetheless, immensely significant for the development and enrichment of Western spirituality and of European intellectual history. For the student of literature and the humanities the writings are also of immense significance in that they form the seedground for ideas and attitudes that exercised an immense and important influence over the development of that movement that we now call the Renaissance. The question of the interpretation of poverty in the writings of Francis is a case in point. One can draw almost a straight cultural line that runs from the writings of Francis on this point, that extends through the most ancient writings that followed his death right down to the allegory of Lady Poverty done by Giotto in the lower church of Assisi and the great hymn to Lady Poverty found in the *Paradiso* of Dante (Canto XII). *Pari Passu*, the same type of line could be drawn from his writing on nature, his teaching on the humanity of Christ, his emphatic treatment of the Passion, etc., and their corresponding treatment in art.

Finally, there is the question of how to classify the writings of Francis. Scholars are not in agreement on this topic and opinions still vary on how to divice his works.[1] In this study, both for the sake of clarity and simplicity, his prose writings are dealt with in the present chapter and the prayers and poetry will be treated in the next. In this section on the prose writings I have followed the most conservative opinions of scholars as to the authenticity of the writings. In the final section of this chapter there will be an addendum that will list the dubious and/or spurious works. It should be noted that only recently has the canon of the writings of the saint received anything like unanimity from scholars. The earliest list of his writings, preserved in a document that dates from about a generation after his death (preserved in Assisi — Mss. Assisi 238) omits some of the writings that we know now to be most certainly authentic (such as the *Rule of 1221*). The great list made by the Irish Franciscan Luke Wadding in the seventeenth century is much more expanded including works that are most certainly spurious. Today, thanks to the work of many scholars of many persuasions dating back for a century or more, there is general agreement about the authentic works even if we still lack complete critical editions of all the works.

I   *The Rules of Life*

It was in the year 1208 that the already converted Francis of Assisi heard the words of the Gospel about the life of poverty in the following of Christ. He left off his former existence of hermit and rebuilder of the church of San Damiano to enter into a life of itinerant preaching. By the following year he had some disciples with him and Francis felt the need to put some organization into the life of his little fraternity. This decision has been recorded in his own words in his *Testament:* "When God gave me some friars, there was no one to tell me what I should do; but the Most High Himself made it clear to me that I must live the life of the Gospel. I had this written down briefly and simply and His Holiness the Pope confirmed it for me."[2] What Francis had written down "briefly" and "simply" is the now lost primitive rule of life of the Franciscan Order. Various attempts have been made to reconstruct that lost rule of life but they must, of necessity, remain conjectural because of the lack of clear documentary evidence. Most scholars do agree, however, that the rule most likely was a *catena* of texts from the Gospel with perhaps some marginal commentary. It is almost certain that the document was not done in any curial or canonical style but was quite rudimentary.[3]

Between 1209 when Pope Innocent III approved this simple rule and 1221 when the rule was rewritten by Saint Francis, momentous events had occurred within his religious fraternity which were to change the friars from a simple band of itinerants into a worldwide movement that had already begun to change the face of both the religion and the culture of the time. Between 1209 and 1221 Clare of

Assisi had already been converted to the following of the Franciscan way of life and was firmly established in Assisi with a large group of feminine followers. Lay people were increasingly more interested in the Franciscan way of life and were beginning to affiliate with it in various ways. The growth of the friars themselves was startling. By the year 1217 bands of friars were living in practically every province of Italy, in France, Spain, Bohemia, Germany, England, and in the Holy Land; by 1219 mission bands of friars were sent to Hungary, Morocco, Tunisia, and Francis himself had made a journey to Syria.

This quick growth of the movement created a whole series of problems both of an administrative and of an ideological nature. It was quite one thing to live out certain ideals of the Gospel with the aid of just a few texts from that Gospel but when the group had reached the size of a few thousand, difficult situations were bound to arise. John Moorman has written that, apart from the inevitable administrative problems of such a group, there were four major areas of unresolved conflict in the Franciscan Order at this period: First was the problem of how to understand and live out the ideal of religious poverty. Secondly, there was the problm of receiving "privileges" from the Vatican. Francis never sought out any canonical privileges for his order; he wanted it to serve at the sufferance and under the obedience of all authority in the Church. In the third place, there was the question of the relationship of priest and layman in the order; Francis himself was not a priest. To admit large numbers of priests into the order not only meant its inevitable clericalization but also again raised the question of total poverty since priests required certain books and appurtenances for the fit exercise of their office. Fourth, and finally, Francis was adamantly opposed to any academic learning; the friar, according to the *Testament* of Saint Francis, was to be *idiota et subditus omnibus* (unlettered and subject to all).[4] Yet in this period the order had already admitted men of considerable learning while others were agitating to go to the universities in order to prepare themselves to evangelize theologically sophisticated groups such as the Cathari who were then engaging the attention of the whole of Christendom.

When Francis arrived back from the Eastern Mission in 1220, events had already happened in his order that caused him severe misgiving: canonical privilege had been given to the friars by the Pope in a letter urging all prelates to receive the friars with honor and to give them the right to preach. The Pope had also forbidden the friars to receive members without a year of trial in the form of a canonical novitiate; nor were friars permitted to wander about without some supervision. Not only that, but when Francis got to Bologna from Venice he found a convent of friars there who were not only in possession of a house but the purpose of the house was for study at the famed university there. According to the early legends, Francis drove the friars from the house physically, cursed the superior, and even put the sick friars out on the street.[5]

It was obvious to Francis by the Michaelmas Chapter of friars held at Assisi in 1221 that some of his ideals had been compromised and that problems had arisen within the ranks of the friars that he had not envisioned when he had written out the short rule in 1209. Accordingly, with the help of Friars Caesar of Speyer and Peter Catani, Francis wrote a new rule that was based on and enlarged from the earlier rule of 1209. This *Rule of 1221*[6] is more commonly called the *Regula Non Bullata* (the unsealed rule) because it was never given the seal *(bulla)* of papal authority. This *Rule of 1221* was obviously an enlargement of the earlier rule (1209) but reflected the many changes that had occurred in the intervening decade.

The *Rule of 1221* is a Latin document that contains a prologue and twenty-three very short chapters. Of these chapters, the first twenty-one are prescriptive obligations for or about the friars and their manner of life, heavily adorned with passages of Sacred Scripture. Chapter twenty-two is an exhortation to the friars and the final chapter is a long prayer.

The *Rule of 1221* is a description of the life that Francis wished to have his friars live in "obedience, without property, and in the state of chastity" (cap. 1). Rules follow for the manner of accepting candidates to the order and rules for the daily routine of the friars. Five chapters (7,8,9,14,15) deal with the exercise of poverty and include strong prohibitions against the use of money and even a prohibition against the use of a horse as a means of travel. Three other rules (16,-17,18) deal with the religious notion of obedience. Other chapters stress the cultivation of Christian virtue (11) and the avoidance of vice, especially sexual irregularity (12,13).

The *Rule of 1221* was evidently not well received by the friars at their convocation in Assisi. The more learned among them thought it diffuse, lacking in legal precision, and incapable in the form in which it had been written of passing muster before the trained legal eyes of the papal curia. Accordingly, there was pressure from the more learned friars and from some of the superiors in the order for Francis to rewrite the *Rule of 1221* into a more acceptable canonical form.

The result of this pressure from within the order was the formulation of the *Rule of 1223*,[7] called the *Regula Bullata* since this *Rule* did get papal approbation in 1223. This *Rule* was dictated by Saint Francis to his companion-secretary Brother Leo who was aided by Brother Bonizo of Bologna, a man trained in the field of canon law.[8] This *Rule* was submitted to the friars for debate and a vote at the Pentecost chapter held at Assisi in the spring of 1223. We do not possess the minutes of that meeting but revisions and emendations of the *Rule* were undoubtedly made. The *Rule* that finally emerged from the debates was approved by Pope Honorius III in November of 1223 and became the official rule of the Friars Minor.

When the *Rule of 1221* and the *Rule of 1223* are compared, it becomes evident, on first examination, that the major difference between the two documents is that the 1223 version is considerably shorter. This is due both to the compression of the language of the later *Rule* as well as to the excision of the many scriptural references that had been included by Caesar of Speyer in the earlier text. Thus the *Rule of 1223* has only twelve chapters (as compared to twenty-three in the *Rule of 1221*) and they may be summarized as follows: (1) The Franciscan life is based on a desire to live the life of the Gospel; (2) the manner of receiving new members; (3) the rules concerning prayer, fasting, and modes of travel; (4) the prohibition regarding the use of money; (5) the rule about the necessity of work; (6) rules on poverty, almsgathering, and the care of sick brethren; (7) on the sacrament of Penance; (8) the role of the Minister General and the convocation of the Pentecost Chapter; (9) regulations for preachers; (10) on the admonition and correction of errant brethren; (11) the relationship of friars and nuns; (12) on missions to the Saracens and other nonbelievers.

The really crucial question about the *Rule of 1223* is whether or not it really reflected the mind and the ideals of Francis or whether it is a compromise document forced on Francis by factions in the order who were not happy with the simple and somewhat primitive life that the early companions of Francis had led.

This question (to which we will return raises the more fundamental question that has really shaped the field of Franciscan studies for nearly a century: Did Francis ever really intend anything like a "religious order" in the traditionally canonical sense of the term or did he seek to found something radically new only to see this effort subverted by the power and influence of the medieval church? This question, first posed by the great Franciscan scholar of the nineteenth century, Paul Sabatier, has colored Franciscan

scholarship to this day. Sabatier's thesis is simply stated: "The movement (i.e. Franciscanism) which ended by being a new family of
monks was at the beginning, antimonastic. To find such contradic-
tions in history is no difficult task. The Gentle Galilean who
preached a personal revelation without dogmatic law or ceremonial
triumphed only to be vanquished for His words were confiscated by
a Church that was essentially sacerdotal and dogmatic."[9]

It is undoubtedly true that Sabatier's thesis was colored by his own
liberal Protestantism but there is also ample evidence that in early
Franciscan history itself there were wide and bitter differences of
opinion about what Francis himself really intended for his followers.
This becomes all the more clear when we compare the differences
between the *Rule of 1221* and the *Rule of 1223* with the Sabatier
thesis in the background. This is not even as difficult as tackling the
vexatious question of the relationship of the *Rules* that we do possess
with the now lost *Primitive Rule* of 1209.

The opinion of the orthodox Franciscan scholars with respect to
the evolution of the rule from its beginning in 1209 to the *Rule of
1223* has been summed up in this way: "In a sense then the Franciscan Order has had but one rule, for the rule of 1221 likewise was
simply the original rule, with additions that were found necessary
during the intervening years, or, to put it another way, the original
rule of 1209, the *First Rule* of 1221, and the *Second Rule* of 1223
were but stages in the development of the rule of the Friars
Minor."[10]

This thesis is sustained by arguing that whatever changes took
place within the legislation written by Francis in 1209, 1221, and
1223 can be explained, not in terms of coercion, but rather in terms
of the actual exigencies that Francis himself saw and to which he
responded. It is further argued that the changes that one can detect
in the various documents, are, for the most part, either editorial or
cosmetic in nature: reduction of the number of the quotes from
Sacred Scripture; conversion of the flat, and somewhat uninspired
prose of Francis; the eliminationof redundancies and repetitions.

Other scholars take a somewhat less optimistic view of the evolution of these documents. They point out that much that was dear to
the heart of Francis was sacrificed in the final revision of the *Rule;*
this was especially true with regard to the practice of absolute poverty. There is evidence that some of the ideas of Francis were softened
and/or mitigated: the famous Gospel texts on renunciation and
poverty (i.e., Matt. 19,21; Luke 9,3: Matt. 16, 24) are completely

missing in the *Rule of 1223*. The Gospel command that nothing was to be taken along on the apostolic journeys that was in chapter 14 of the *Rule of 1221* was excised from the revised rule by a decision of the ministers. The obligation of friars to go on foot and to avoid the use of horses is omitted as is the obligation to live as poor as Christ and the Blessed Virgin (cap. 9 in the *Rule of 1221*). Finally, the obligation of a new postulant to the order to give up all his worldly goods upon the entrance to the order is amended and softened in the *Rule of 1223* with the coda "if they are unable to do this then their good intention will suffice." (cap. 2)

It seems obvious that the *Rule of 1223* has lost some of the un-lettered and naive simplicity of the earlier legislation; the Latin of the later *Rule* is much more elegant and controlled. The harshness of the interpretation of poverty is also mitigated. While the judgment of John Moorman that the *Rule of 1223* is suffused with the spirit of Saint Francis is undoubtedly correct,[11] it seems likewise true that the *Rule of 1223* cannot be said to have the same spirit as the primitive rule of 1209 nor is it completely consonant with the evangelical rigor of the *Rule of 1221*. The Sabatier thesis may be greatly exaggerated but there is more than a grain of truth in it. A close reading of early Franciscan legislation shows an undoubted growth of routinization and legalism.

This labored discussion and comparison of two rather dull ecclesiastical documents may strike one who is neither a Franciscan nor a medievalist as being a bit excessive, but the early Franciscan rules, humble enough documents in themselves, had a profound and lasting effect on medieval culture, and, indeed, it has been suggested by some scholars of high repute that this medieval dispute over the Franciscan style of life has had reverberations down to the modern period.

It must be remembered that, if there are still disagreements today about the mind of Francis as it is reflected in the early legislation, this is a dispute that existed from the very first days of the Franciscan movement. After the acceptance of the *Rule of 1223* by the friars and its later ratification by papal authority there were still acrimonious debates about the meaning of the specific rules and, more especially, how the *Rule* was to be read with specific reference to the question of the observance of evangelical poverty. After the death of Francis (in 1226) a bitter struggle broke out that was to last for over a cen-tury. Some of his oldest companions and others inflamed by his ideals held to a strict view of poverty and attached this ascetic ideal to the ideas of Joachim of Flora, a Calabrian monk and mystic who had lived some years before Francis. Joachim had predicted a New Age of the Spirit and many of the rigorist friars were convinced that Francis, who stood in such startling contrast to the old order of the church, was the man who had ushered in this new age of love and the Spirit. These friars looked with askance at the rapid transformation of the brotherhood of Friars Minor into an institutionalized structure of religious not unlike the traditional monastic groups that had existed prior to the time when Francis was active. Within a year or two after the death of Francis a huge church was begun at Assisi which was to serve as a shrine for the man who was canonized only two years after his death (1228). Franciscan friars quickly invaded the universities and soon held professorial chairs at the leading educational centers. In short, the vagrant and mendicant spirit of the original brotherhood found itself in the process of being transformed into a property-bound and somewhat static religious establishment.

The Conventuals, who maintained an upper hand in the administration of the order, did everything they could to stamp out the spirit of the Spirituals (the name for the older and more conservative members of the Franciscans) whom they regarded as heretics and revolutionary fanatics little distinguishable from other left wing groups of religious revolutionaries then common all over the face of Europe. The General Chapter of the Franciscans in 1260 decided to have John of Fidanza (Saint Bonaventure) write an official life of Francis and also ordered the suppression of all older legends and stories of the saint in an effort to stem the constant appeal to the "real" Francis and his view of poverty. By the fourteenth century efforts to stamp out the Spiritual party had reached such a fever pitch that in 1318 four dissident friars, who belonged to the Spiritual wing of the Franciscans, were sent to the stake at Marseilles. The battle did not end there and active campaigning against the Spirituals went on through most of the century.

It would not be germane to the main topic of this study to try and sort out all of the motivations nor to try and justify one side or the other in this most bitter of battles. What is of importance for us, however, is to realize that the vision of Francis, and especially as this vision was understood by the Spiritual wing of the Franciscans, did not simply die out as a visible and viable religious movement with the demise of the Spirituals. The Spirituals belonged to a large current of medieval religious ideas that had flourished in Europe in the late middle ages (e.g., the Poor Men of Lyons, the followers of

Peter Waldo). This current was characterized by strong social views, a strain of apocalypticism, a desire for, and exaltation of, poverty, and an unshakeable conviction that the powers of this world, both ecclesiastical and civil, would be brought down in judgment. Francis, and the ideals that he stood for, was a rallying point for many who swam in this current. The arguments and battles over what Francis meant by the "following of the teaching and in the footsteps of Our Lord Jesus Christ" (cap. 1, *Rule of 1221*) did not end with the triumph of the Conventuals. There is some evidence that the so-called Radical Reformation that broke out within a year or two of Luther's break with Rome was fed by many of the ideas that had been discussed and acted upon in the swirling controversies about the mind of Francis on the nature of the evangelical life. Thus, it would not be a total exaggeration to say that such radical reformers as Thomas of Muntzer were, in fact, descendants of the Spiritual Franciscans. Indeed, Professor Friedrich Heer has suggested that the "author of the Magdeburg Centuries and all the revolutionary spiritualists right down to the nineteenth century looked on Francis as their progenitor."[12]

Before ending this section on the various *Rules* written by Saint Francis, brief mention should be made of the short *Forma Vivendi* (i.e., mode of living or rule of life) that Francis wrote for the religious community of women who lived under the leadership of Clare of Assisi, one of the earliest converts to the Franciscan style of life and one of the closest friends that Francis had. Clare of Assisi mentions in her own *Testament* that Francis wrote often to the sisters.[13] However, only two of these writings have survived the centuries and been preserved: a short *Testament* (to be discussed later in this chapter) written just before his death and what must be judged either to be an encapsulated version of a longer *Rule* or merely an exhortation of sorts. Its brevity permits us to quote it in its entirety:

> Because it was God who inspired you to become daughters and handmaids of the Most High Supreme King and Father in heaven and to espouse yourselves to the Holy Spirit by choosing to live according to the perfection of the Holy Gospel, I desire and promise you personally and in the name of my friars that I will always have the same loving care special solicitude for you as for them.[14]

This brief statement was called a "formula of life" by Pope Gregory IX in a letter to Blessed Agnes of Prague and Clare of Assisi uses the same phrase in her own writings. The short statement should be seen as a crystallized statement of the pursuit of perfection for women religious as seen through the eyes of Francis: a spiritual marriage to the Holy Trinity in order to live in conformity to the Gospel with the continued solicitude and care of the "little brothers" *(fratres minores)* who seek the same perfection.

II   The Rule For Hermitages

It is important to remember that the very first followers of Saint Francis had no fixed abodes in the form of convents or monasteries. In fact, the *Rule of 1223* expressly forbade the friars to possess houses or plots of ground. The early friars were expected to work at humble occupations to support themselves and to beg when there was no work (cf. cap. 7 *Rule of 1221* and cap. 5 of *Rule of 1223*) and it was expected that they would find shelter near the hospitals, leprosaria, etc., where they were to find their employment. They were, in short, wanderers. Saint Francis also expected the friars to preach and exhort the people in their journey and after these tours the friars were encouraged to return to the environs of Assisi for a period of quiet and contemplation. Thomas of Celano in both of his Lives of the Saint mentions that Francis and his companions retired to various out-of-the-way spots for periods of retreat and contemplation.

This eremetical and contemplative strain in the Franciscan life is quite consistent with the whole development of Francis's own spiritual life. After he had made his final break with family ties in Assisi (early in 1206) Francis spent the next three years in the life of solitude; it was recorded that he wore a kind of "hermit's dress, with a leather girdle about his waist; he carried a staff in his hands and wore shoes on his feet."[15] Again, after the approval of the rule in 1209, Francis and his companions seriously discussed whether or not they should lead a life of strict eremitism or engage in the active life of wandering preachers. Any number of times Thomas of Celano mentions the friars as spending time away from crowds and on retreats, usually in remote areas. The great retreat of Francis on Mount La Verna (a place given to the friars for the purpose of seclusion) was the occasion of the stigmata in 1224. Even to this day visitors to Assisi may climb the side of Mt. Subasio and visit the small friary called the *Carceri* (lit. the prison) which is the site of one of the oldest Franciscan eremetical retreats.

As with much of the writing of Francis, it is most difficult to judge just when he wrote the short document called *The Rule For Hermitages*. Facchinetti, following other authorities, believes that it was in existence before 1218;[16] the editors of the *Omnibus* put the date at 1223 because the document uses the word *custos* (designating a superior of a province) which, while in use as early as 1217, did not get into the *Rule of 1221* but appeared after that date as a technical term in Franciscan legal terminology.[17] There is no doubt at all among scholars that it is an authentic work of Francis.[18]

The Rule For Hermitages in itself is quite short, consisting in translation of about four or five paragraphs. It directs that only three or four friars at a time should go off on retreat and a number of these (say, two of them) should act as "mothers" to the remainder. There should be a rule of silence and common prayer at stipulated times of day according to the canonical hours. Those who act as the "mothers" should assure those on retreat the requisite silence and sustenance needed to insure the sense of solitude and separation so vital for the contemplative enterprise. Outsiders should be kept away from the eremetical enclosure by those who serve as the "mothers." In the course of time there should be a reversal of rules, the "mothers" becoming the "sons" and vice versa. This can be done "according to whatever arrangement seems best suited for the moment."[19]

Thomas Merton has commented on the religious genius of this short document. According to Merton, Francis attempted to bridge the ancient and austere tradition of individual ascesis that goes all the way back to the desert fathers of Egypt with the warm and fraternal bond of community that so suffused the early Franciscan spirit.[20] Francis wanted, then, to combine the tradition of solitary contemplation that he himself had practiced at the beginning of his own spiritual life with the life of an apostolic and wandering brotherhood living in a spirit of fraternal union.

But the *Rule for Hermitages* is not only significant because of its importance for the life of contemplatives in the Catholic tradition. The very fact that Francis wrote such a rule indicated a hidden ambivalence in Franciscan life, an ambivalence that was only resolved after a long struggle within the order itself. Francis conceived of his life and the life of his followers as being that of itinerancy. He was quite content to travel and to stop where providence stopped him. But another side of him thirsted for a place to use for religious retirement. As Cajetan Esser notes: "that tendency towards the contemplative life, which right from the beginning was a characteristic of the Franciscan movement was another force that introduced a certain degree of permanence or stability."[21] Thus the *Rule For Hermitages* gave witness to a strain in Franciscanism that was more interested in place than movement; in the course of its long history it was this desire for place that was to come to prominence and, finally, to prevail. Today, for example, one finds Franciscans in schools, colleges, parishes, chaplancies, and other posts; one finds very few, if any, on the road, living as mendicants or by the labor of their hands. It is also worth noting that in the days of the struggles of the Spirituals and the Conventuals, the Spirituals greatly emphasized the contemplative and retiring side of the Franciscan life. The friars who settled in the Marches around Ancona in Northern Italy (and from whose number the *Fioretti* was to appear in the fourteenth century) separated themselves almost completely from the larger world and led an almost completely eremetical life in the forests of that part of Italy. Even the Conventuals did not lose the spirit of retirement. We must remember that Saint Bonaventure wrote his great mystical treatise the *Itinerarium Mentis ad Deum* not in the bustle of the University of Paris but while in retreat at the mountain convent of La Verna.

III *The* Admonitions

In the years after the approval of the *Primitive Rule* (1209) by Pope Innocent III there were annual gatherings of the friars at the church of the Portiuncula (lit. the "little portion"; it was also called Saint Mary of the Angels) at the time of Michaelmas and Pentecost. These annual meetings, called chapters, were stipulated both in the *Rule of 1221* and the *Rule of 1223* but antedated these Rules by some years. During the lifetime of Saint Francis we know that he took advantage of these gatherings of his brethren to exhort and instruct them on any number of topics. Thus the author of the *Legend of the Three Companions* writes that at these chapters "Saint Francis exhorted the brothers, reprimanding what was blameworthy, and directing them as he was inspired of the Spirit of God. In all he said he spoke lovingly, and carried out what he preached in his own actions."[22] Scholars that generally agree it was from these extemporaneous exhortations that the collection now called the *Admonitions* took its origin. Scholars further agree that the compilation of these sayings was more than likely made and edited into its present form some time after the death of the saint. There is, however, scholarly consensus that the collection must be attributed directly to the saint and that it faithfully reflects his own mind and spirit. Indeed, J. Cambell insists that the attribution of these writings to Francis are *les mieux defendus* of all of his writings and reflect usages (especially in the citation of the Scriptures) that are totally consonant with what we know of the style of Francis.[23]

The *Admonitions* contains twenty-eight small sections that range over a broad number of topics concerning the spiritual life of the friars. Some of these exhortations, such as the first one on the Holy Eucharist, bear a great similarity to the medieval-style catena sermon in that they contain a few original sentences of the author and then a whole chain *(catena)* of texts from Holy Scripture. These biblical quotations are woven into the very fabric of the exhortations themselves. Beginning with exhortation#14 there are a whole series of meditations on the Sermon on the Mount but aside from this theme there does not seem to be any internal consistency or unifying theme to the *Admonitions*. A quotation from any one of the *Admonitions* gives a good feel for the style of all of them:

> Saint Paul tells us 'No one can say Jesus is Lord except in the Spirit'' (I Cor. 12, 3) and, 'There is no one who does good, no, not even one' (Rom. 3, 12). And so when a man envies his brother the good that God does or says through him it is like committing a sin of blasphemy, because it is really envying God, who is the source of every good.[24]

Of all the *Admonitions* the one that is the most interesting, at least from the point of view of style, is #27 which, unlike the turgid Latin prose of the others, is written in a near poetic style not unlike the prayers that have also come down to us from Francis. There is no rhyme scheme to these lines but there is an antithetical parallelism in the presentation that is reminiscent of Hebrew poetry. Thus:

> Where there is love and wisdom
> there is neither fear nor ignorance
> where there is patience and humility
> there is neither anger nor annoyance
>   etc.

This admonition seems similar in style and tone to a prayer often attributed to Saint Francis (Lord, make me an instrument of thy peace/where there is hatred, let me sow love, etc.). It may well be that this particular admonition was the remote source of that prayer which is not from the pen of the saint but which can be traced back no earlier than the first part of this century.

The *Admonitions* are important in Franciscan thought not because of their intrinsic beauty nor because of their great originality as spiritual documents; they are important because they do provide an ancient gloss, from the pen of Francis, on the written rules that have been so important in the history of the Franciscan Order. They reflect some of the major preoccupations of Francis and the early friars. Cajetan Esser, the noted Franciscan scholar, has singled out the *Admonitions* as a hitherto neglected area of research in the yet uncompleted study of the mind and ideals of Francis in the earliest and most formative years of the Franciscan Order.[25] It will be the task of further research, Esser notes, to correlate the spirituality of the *Admonitions* with the mind of Saint Francis as it was expressed in his other writings, and especially in the *Rules* and the *Testament* in order to create a true composite of the saint's spirituality.

Twenty-eight of these admonitions have come down to us and they are each listed with a heading; it is evident from the titles of each of the *Admonitions* that there is no progressive uniformity or thematic unity. They form, rather, an anthology of exhortations that were delivered by the saints over a number of years and in varying circumstances. The headings of *Admonitions* in their proper order are as follows: (1) The Blessed Sacrament, (2) The Evil of Self Will, (3) Perfect and Imperfect Obedience, (4) No One Should Claim the Office of Superior as His Own, (5) No One Should Give Way to Pride but Boast Only in the Cross of the Lord, (6) The Imitation of Christ, (7) Good Works Must Follow Knowledge, (8) Beware the Sin of Envy, (9) Charity, (10) Exterior Mortification, (11) No One Should Be Scandalized at Another's Fall, (12) How to know the Spirit of God, (13) Patience, (14) Poverty of Spirit, (15) The Peacemakers, (16) Purity of Heart, (17) The Humble Religious, (18) Compassion for One's Neighbor, (19) The Happy and Unhappy Religious, (20) The Virtuous and Happy Religious, (21) The Happy and the Frivolous Religious, (22) The Talkative Religious, (23) True Correction, (24) True Humility, (25) True Love, (26) Religious Should Be Respectful Towards the Clergy, (27) Virtue and Vice, and (28) Virtue Should Be Concealed or it Will be Lost.

IV *The Testaments*

In the very last months of his life, Francis dictated what has been called by one Franciscan scholar "the most moving of all his works, by its very simplicity, an appeal more touching than all the Rules and Admonitions."[26] Undoubtedly reflecting on the past work and concerned about the future of his friars, he left them a final testament. This *Testament* is part autobiography, part a personal confession of faith, and part a stern exhortation to his followers and disciples. The *Testament* does not follow a logically developed pattern but the document can be broken down into the following parts: an autobiographical reminiscence; an act of faith; the recollection of the early friars; a strong exhortation against the acceptance of privilege; a plea for the friars to obey their superiors; a demand that they always accept the rule of life; and, finally, a closing blessing.

Francis begins the *Testament* by recalling his early conversion; it is one of the few references that he ever made to his own person and life: "When I was still a sinner I thought it a bitter thing to look upon a leper and the Lord led me to them and taught me to be merciful."[27] Francis then continued by saying that "I tarried a bit and then left the world." Following this piece of autobiography, Francis professes his great respect for the priests of the Church and his acceptance of their authority, in the Holy Eucharist, and in the preachers and teachers of the Church.

In the next part of the *Testament* he recalls the early days of the brotherhood of the friars. His companions were "entrusted to him by the Lord" and he, not knowing how to guide them, found God revealing what manner of life they should lead in the Gospel and it was written down in "a few words." This, of course, is a reference to the now lost primitive rule. In those days, Francis recalled, the friars were content with a patched habit; they said their prayers assiduously; they were subject to all men; they worked with their hands and when there was no work, they went out like the poor and begged for their sustenance. In short, they lived a life of wayfarers and pilgrims.

Francis abruptly shifts from this stream of reminiscence to make an "imperative demand of obedience" that no friar seek out any papal privilege either by himself or through an intermediary. He then exhorts obedience on the part of the friars and suggests means by which the order can deal with recalcitrant friars.

In the final section of the *Testament* Francis exhorts his brothers to neither add nor subtract to what he had written and to keep this *Testament* and read it along with the reading of the *Rule*. He forbade any tortuous interpretations of the *Rule* or any glosses on it. In the very last paragraph Francis extends his blessing to all the brethren and prays that those who keep his words will be filled with the heavenly benedictions of God.

The *Testament* had a great deal of authority in the early Franciscan movement. Both Thomas of Celano and Saint Bonaventure, in their respective lives of the saint, quote from it verbatim. Inevitably, an early controversy arose about whether or not the *Testament* had binding and legal authority on the friars. Francis had insisted in the *Testament* that the friars live the *Rule* literally and without gloss. The General Council of the Franciscans, held in 1230, some four years after the death of Francis, debated the legal status of the *Testament* and finally referred the question of the binding nature of the *Testament* to Pope Gregory IX for his opinion and his decision.

Gregory's answer came in the papal bull *Quo Elongati* (September, 1230). Gregory paid tribute to Saint Francis (whom he had known personally and admired) but said that the *Testament* could not be regarded as binding in character since Francis had acted on his own without benefit of the counsel of the ministers of the order. Gregory further noted that the part of the *Rule* which stated that the friars should live without any possessions of their own *(sine proprio)* could not be taken in any literal sense. Gregory introduced the nice legal fiction that the properties and other material possessions of the friars would be owned by the Vatican and the friars then could have the use and the benefit of these things without actually owning them. This perfectly legal idea (founded in the old Roman law of *ususfructus*) was an impeccable compromise to avoid a nasty intramural dispute in the Franciscan Order. But it would also seem that it subverted the intention of Francis himself by effectively destroying the wandering brotherhood, utterly dependent on the providence of God, which he had first envisioned.

Some writers — notably Paul Sabatier — have viewed the *Testament* as a last ditch effort on the part of Francis to subvert the *Rule of 1223* which had been thrust upon him, and so to return to the primitive ideals of the *Rule of 1209*. It seems difficult to see that this can be proved from a reading of the *Testament;* that is not apparently the intention of the saint. What does seem abundantly clear is that at least part of his motive in the *Testament* was to exercise his personal authority to halt the erosion of his ideals and to hold in check the increasing mitigations and routinization of the ideals of poverty that he had originally set out. It is quite significant that the rigorist wing of the Franciscans (including the Spirituals) used the

Testament as a powerful weapon in their battle against what they saw as the laxity and the weakening of the original ideals of the saint in the life style and philosophy of the Conventuals.

It would be too strong to suggest, as did Sabatier, that this *Testament* was designed to subvert the *Rule of 1223*. The text, as I suggested earlier, will not support such an interpretation. Nonetheless, there is great urgency in this document, an urgency that seems to me to reflect the concern of the saint with the further erosion of his ideals:

No brother should say "This is another rule"; for this is a testament, a memorial, an exhortation, and a remembrance that I, Brother Francis, have made for you my blessed brothers so that you will be better able to observe the holy rule that we have promised before the Lord. The minister general and all the other ministers and guardians are obliged by obedience to neither add nor subtract from these words. In fact, they should carry a copy of this along with the Rule, and in all meetings when they read the rule, this also should be read. All my brothers, clerical and lay, are ordered in obedience to make glosses neither on this rule nor on these words; neither should they say, "This should be interpreted thusly"; rather, as the Lord told me what to say and how to write this rule simply and purely, they are to observe this rule and these words simply and purely and fulfill them right to the end.[28]

Besides this *Testament* some of the early sources (notably the *Speculum Majus* and the *Compilatio Perusina*) record that just a few months before his death Francis called for the priest Benedict of Prato while he was sick in bed and dictated a blessing for those who were in the order at that time and for all who would join their ranks in the future. He says that since he was so weak and sick (the *Speculum Majus* says that he had hemorrhaged the entire night before) he wanted to leave his friars three basic thoughts and obligations: "Always love each other; always love Our Lady, Holy Poverty; always be faithful to the prelates and clerics of Holy Mother the Church."[29]

The text is quite short but completely consistent with the thought and the style of the saint. One should note that this short text does express, in a very few words, some basic themes expressed at greater length in other of the writings of Francis: fraternal love; obedience to the authority of the Church; and devotion to the ideal of poverty. It is for this reason that, despite the absence of this story in the early

Lives of the saint, it is regarded by most authorities as an authentic part of the corpus of the writings of Francis.[30]

Along with this *Little Testament,* as it is often called, the ancient sources have also preserved a last expression of the saint *(ultima voluntas)* written by Francis in the last months of his life for the nuns who lived at Assisi under the aegis of Clare of Assisi. We cannot date the last statement to the Poor Clares more precisely; it is generally agreed that it was written during the last sickness of the saint. Again, it is a very brief document, and in its compressed form, manages to express the constant preoccupation of the last days of the saint: the maintenance of his ideals. The brevity of the statement permits us to quote it in full:

I, little brother Francis, wish to live according to the life and poverty of our Most High Lord Jesus Christ and His Most Holy Mother and to persevere in this to the last. And I beseech you, my ladies, and I exhort you to live always in this most holy life and poverty. Keep close watch over yourselves so that you never abandon it through the teaching or advice of anyone.[31]

V   *The Letters of Saint Francis*

The ancient sources and legends speak not infrequently of Saint Francis writing or dictating letters. Many of these letters have been lost in the course of time and those letters that have survived or those that have been ascribed to him have been the source of some scholarly debate. Even today there is some disagreement about the authentic corpus of his letters. In this section we will deal only with those letters that all scholars accept as authentic and relegate to a mere mention those that are still the object of scholarly dispute.

The most interesting letter of the ones that surely come from Francis is the letter to Brother Leo. Its contents, are of slight significance but what is important is that it is one of two autographs that we possess of the saint. This particular letter is preserved as a relic in the Cathedral of Spoleto. The autograph is not only important as an historical and religious relic but also because it shows quite clearly that Francis, rather like Shakespeare, had "little Latin." The letter, undoctored by a secretarial hand, shows the flat style, the repeated conjunctions, and the awkward grammar of an unsteady Latinist.

The letter itself, consisting of only a few short lines, alludes to a journey that Leo and Francis had taken together. Francis desired to "sum up" what they had talked about on that journey. In essence, he advised Leo to follow God's will as closely as he could in living the life of poverty. He then added that if Leo needed more clarification or "for your consolation," he was welcome to come to Francis for further discussion.[32] Since Leo was a constant companion and served as secretary to Francis in the latter's final years the letter seems to have been written when they were not in constant communication. Scholars, not without some hesitancy, usually date it before 1220. More precise dating does not seem to be possible.

The Letter to All the Faithful is a much more lengthy and interesting document. It was written as a circular letter and, according to John Moorman, was probably read out loud by the friars when they were on their preaching journey.[33] In the circular Francis alludes to the fact that he was too ill to travel himself. This is the only chronological clue in the letter; from the allusion to the illness, it would seem that it should be dated either around 1215 or during the last period of his life (1224 - 26). Based solely on internal evidence, the later dating does seem preferable since the themes of this letter bear close resemblance to the ideas that are expressed in the *Testament* and in the *Letter to All Clerics*, both of which date from the later period of his life.

The Letter to All the Faithful contains a series of exhortations and admonitions that were dear to the heart and mind of Francis and were also treated in the *Admonitions*, the *Rule of 1221*, and in the *Testament*: Reverence for the Sacrament of the Holy Eucharist; the necessity of confession and penance; respect for the Sacred Mysteries of the Church and their ministers; the need for the virtue of simplicity and purity of heart. The letter makes abundant use of texts from Sacred Scripture, is written with a certain elegance of style (and hence an editorial hand is suspected), and, unlike most of the prose pieces of Francis, makes use of a homely illustration (that of a dying man) to strengthen a point about the need for repentance. It is the only time in his writings that such an illustration is used. The fact that there is an homiletic device in the letter strengthens the hypothesis that it was meant to be a preaching device to be read to a largely illiterate audience. If that be the case, then it also serves as a good example of the style of short sermon that a medieval audience might be expected to hear. The end of the letter includes an injunction for copies to be made and circulated and a plea to have the letter read to those who were unable to read it for themselves. This again would testify to the general pastoral nature of the letter.[34]

The Letter to All Clerics is very similar in style to the *Letter to All the Faithful*. This letter, which in some early manuscripts is called *De Reverentia Corporis Domini* (On Reverencing the Body of the Lord) does not have the salutation "to all the clerics of the world" in the earlier codices and is treated by some as a document similar to the *Religious Life in a Hermitage*.[35] Despite the dispute as to where to classify it (and my own judgment is that it should be treated as a circular letter) there is unanimity in ascribing it to Francis. Given the topic that it treats, one should also place it in the later period of the life of Francis when he was preoccupied with the sacrament of the Holy Eucharist.

The Letter to All Clerics is quite short (consisting of only four paragraphs and a final exhortation to have the letter copied and circulated) and it deals with a subject that Francis treated not only in his writings but that occupied his attention in his earliest days of residence at San Damiano: the care and maintenance of sacred things. Francis exhorts the readers of this letter to provide decorous places for the celebration of the Holy Eucharist (perhaps remembering his own attempts to restore the church of San Damiano); to use only decorous and clean utensils in the celebration of the Mass; always to exercise due reverence. Francis even insists that "God's name and His written words should be picked up if they are found lying in the dirt, and put into a suitable place." This latter injunction is one more small clue as to the importance of symbolic action in the mind set of the saint. One has reverence for the word of God even in its manufactured expression; one never uses the creatures of the natural world because they are signs or symbols of God.[36]

There are three other letters safely ascribed to the pen of Saint Francis that can be classified as circular letters, meant for a larger public: *Letter to a General Chapter;* the *Letter to All the Friars;* the *Letter to All the Superiors,* plus *The Letter to All the Rulers of the People;* the last mentioned of disputed authenticity.

All of these letters have certain common characteristics: they were obviously meant to be circularized by means of copies that were to be made of the originals (this was a common final exhortation in the letters) or by reading the letter out loud to larger groups. All of the letters are probably datable from the last period of the saint's life, a time when he was unable to travel as far and as long as he wished, due to the recurrent bouts of illness and because of his progressive blindness. The theme of these letters tends to be the same: exhortations to an increased effort in the life of holiness and prayer; reverence for the Holy Eucharist; remembrance that the end of man is to find God.

The *Letter to All the Rulers* is typical in this regard.[37] It contains four sections: a greeting from "Brother Francis, your poor worthless servant" followed by exhortations to keep the commandments of God and to honor Him worthily in the Holy Eucharist. The final paragraph blesses those who will keep a copy of the letter which he has written: "those who keep a copy of this letter and put its prescriptions into practice can rest asssured that they have God's blessing."

The *Letter to a General Chapter*, the *Letter to All the Friars*, and the *Letter to All the Superiors* are, as the titles indicate, missives for various parts of the Franciscan family. Again, there is no way to date these letters accurately, but from some internal references it is safe to say that they date from the last years of the saint's life, years in which problems and challenges from within the order would prompt much of this correspondence. There is nothing striking or literary about these documents but they are important in their own way for the reconstruction of early Franciscan history.

The *Letter to a General Chapter*[38] must have been written some time after 1223 since the letter says that clerics are bound to the recitation of the Canonical Hours; it was the earlier practice for all the friars to do this and the restrictive note that this was an obligation of clerics must reflect the legislation of the *Rule of 1223*. Since some of the manuscripts say that this was a letter for a *General* chapter, that could mean that the letter was written before the chapter of 1224 but if the letter was simply destined for one of the many provincial or regional chapters then we can only say that the letter was after 1223 and leave it at that. Ubertino da Casale's *Arbor Vitae Crucifixae* (written in 1305) simply says that the letter was written in the last days of the life of Saint Francis and we must leave the dating that vague, i.e., sometime after 1223.

The letter is a strong exhortation for the friars to celebrate the Office and the Mass with proper deference and a sense of great holiness. Each of the sections begins with an impassioned phrase of appeal: "Listen then, Sons of God and my friars"; "Listen to this, my friar brothers"; "Remember then your dignity, my friar priests"; etc. The object of this exhortatory exercise is easily summarized by

Francis in his charge to the Minister General in the latter part of the letter: ". . . see that the Rule is observed inviolably by all and that the clerics say the Office devoutly, not concentrating on the melody of the chant, but being careful that their hearts are in harmony so that their words may be in harmony with their hearts and their hearts with God."

There is one injunction in the *Letter to a General Chapter* that is difficult to interpret and that has a certain importance for the history of liturgical practice at that time. Francis wrote that "in the places where the friars live only one Mass a day be said in the rite of the holy church. If there are several priests in the place, each should be glad for the love of charity to have assisted at the celebration of the other." Does that mean that Francis was forbidding the celebration of private masses by priest friars and encouraging only one conventual mass to be said at each friary? We know that the custom of private masses was well established at this period. That question is hard to answer; some scholars have interpreted the passage to mean that there was to be only one mass at the friary. Others point out that in this period the Mass according to the Roman Rite was an extremely long and complicated rite with additions and ceremonies that had grown exponentially over the centuries. Thus, some think that Francis meant that there was only to be one Mass according to the Roman Rite and that the private celebration of Mass (which was shorter and allowed for more spontaneity) could be celebrated at the friars' leisure. There is no way to answer satisfactorily that question here but it would not be out of place to indicate at least that the early Franciscan movement was to have an immense impact on the development of the Roman liturgy, a development that would be halted only when the celebration of the Mass was put into a form of stringent uniformity at the time of the Council of Trent in the sixteenth century.[39]

The *Letter to All the Superiors of the Friars Minor*[40] repeats a theme that Saint Francis had written about in his *Testament* and in the *Letter to a General Chapter:* the proper devotion due to the Holy Eucharist. It is worth noting that in this regard Francis departs from his usual stringent attitude about poverty and enjoins the superiors to "set the greatest value, too, on chalices, corporals, and all the ornaments of the altar that are related to the Holy Sacrifice." Francis, in that same paragraph, also enjoins the superiors to remove the Holy Eucharist from any poor place and take it where the surroundings are worthy; he also recommends due reverence for the written word of God. After a final exhortation to preach penance to the people, the saint concludes the letter by promising God's blessing to those who "copy and keep it, and have copies made for the friars who are devoted to preaching or are superiors. . . ."

The *Letter to a Minister*[41] is one of the few examples of a personal epistle that has come down to us from the hand of the saint, the others being the *Letter to Brother Leo* (already discussed) and the disputed letters to *Brother Anthony* and to *Jacopa da Settesoli*. A few of the manuscripts entitle this letter to "the minister general" but this is hardly likely. The subject of the letter is the care and discipline of unruly friars. Saint Francis counsels love toward these brothers and gently hints that retirement to a hermitage (evidently the solution proposed by the superior) was not to be encouraged. Since Saint Francis mentions in the letter that the forthcoming Pentecost Chapter would make one chapter on the subject of mortal sin instead of the many already existent it can be assumed that the letter was written after the writing of the *Rule of 1221* and before the codification of the new rule. The letter ends with an injunction that the recipient attend the chapter with his friars; this command would preclude its intended recipient being Brother Elias since, as the general of the order, he would not only have been expected to attend the chapter but preside over it. We must then conclude that the letter was meant for some provincial superior.

VI   *Disputed Prose Works of Francis*

When Father Luke Wadding, a seventeenth-century Irish Franciscan, compiled the works that he thought came from the pen of Francis his list was far longer than any that would be accepted in our own time.[42] His pioneering effort at establishing the works of Francis went through many editions but was not subjected to close historical scrutiny until the second half of the nineteenth century. Today, as a result of nearly a century of historical scholarship, a near consensus among scholars holds many of the items on Wadding's list to be spurious. Thus it would be unnecessary to discuss the sayings, collations, proverbs, prayers, and prophecies that once made up a part of his list.

Two of the documents that we have already discussed in this chapter are still debated as regards their authenticity: the *Letter to All the Rules* is admitted by some scholars as a genuine letter of Francis (and we have followed that judgment) while others still have doubts about it.[43] It is not listed in the most ancient compilations of the writings of Francis nor is it alluded to in the early chronicles. However, an early history of the Franciscan Order, written by one of the minister generals of the order, records an old story that says that a thirteenth-century friar, Giovanni Parenti, had an autograph of the letter and that he had carried it to Spain where it had been kept for a long period before it was lost. On the basis of this tradition and internal evidence many are inclined to accept its authenticity.[44]

Similarly, the *Letter to All Clerics* (which we have also discussed in this chapter) is questioned. It has a very sketchy manuscript history and was not even known until Paul Sabatier published a version of it from a codex that he had found in a library in Volterra, Italy. Because of its similarity in theme to other letters written later in the saint's life, it is generally accepted as authentic.[45]

There are two other letters, which we have not discussed, about which there is still considerable controversy: The *Letter to Saint Anthony* and the *Letter to Frate Jacopa dei Settesoli*. The point at issue in both cases is not whether Francis wrote to these people (we know that he did in both cases) but whether the letters that have come down to us are, in fact, the letters that he sent.

We know from Thomas of Celano that Francis had written a letter to Anthony, a brilliant young theologian, in answer to Anthony's request to teach theology to this fellow friar. What is very much in dispute is whether or not the letter that has come down to us is, in fact, the letter that Francis sent. This question has not yet been answered to anyone's complete satisfaction. Recently two eminent theologians and critics (Esser and Bonmann) again reexamined the whole question and reached contradictory conclusions even though the weight of opinion seems not to favor the authenticity of the letter.[46] The letter, which gives Anthony permission to teach theology as long as this study does not "extinguish the spirit of prayer and devotion," is consonant with what we know of the episode; but there is still no "objectively valid argument to prove that St. Francis wrote that particular letter."[47]

The circumstances surrounding the *Letter to Jacopa dei Settesoli* are similar to those of the *Letter to Saint Anthony*. Jacopa was a noble Roman matron and a close friend of Francis. She was with him during the last days of his life, called there, according to the sources, by Francis himself. It is recorded (for example, in the *Legend of the Three Companions*[48]) that he wrote a note to her asking that she come in haste and try to get there before a Saturday; she was further requested to bring some cloth for his shroud, some candles for his funeral rites, and a bit of sweet food that she had once given him during an illness in Rome. The letter that is supposed to come from this incident can be traced no further back than a century after the death of Francis so that in the judgment of most scholars there is no guarantee that the letter is the actual text of what Francis wrote; it may be only a paraphrase of his thought as it was taken from the biographical sources[49]; for this reason the letter is not accepted as an authentic work of the saint.

Some other minor pieces that in the past were ascribed to the saint are not so accepted today. Besides the three pieces described above as doubtfully authentic in their present form (i.e., the *Letter to All the Rulers*, the *Letter to Jacopa*, and perhaps the *Letter to Saint Anthony*), there is an old prayer called the "Prayer before the Crucifix at San Damiano" which is not accepted as authentic in its present form. Finally, three smaller pieces are listed by Jacques Cambell as simply "quelques écrits apocryphes": the *Letter of Obedience to Brother Agnello*; the prayer "Absorbeat"; and a paraphrase of the *Lord's Prayer*.[50]

VII　*The Significance of the Prose Works*

The noted Franciscan scholar, Lothar Hardick, once wrote some very instructive words on the beginning of the Franciscan movement:

> The life of Saint Francis was for that first period the only Rule that his little flock possessed. Of this there can be no doubt. He had become the literal follower of Jesus Christ. But whosoever walks so closely in the way of Christ will himself have followers who will take his ideals as the pattern of their life. So it was in the beginning of the Order: the Franciscan life simply grew out of the life of Saint Francis. By the very nature of things, of course, such an ideal could not last for long in so simple a form. But until the brotherhood grew in numbers, Francis felt no need to multiply rules, to encompass himself or his brothers with too definite a plan. The Franciscan life was simply his life, the life that God had revealed to him, the life of simple union with God. Even when the Order grew and a written rule became a necessity, the life of Francis remained, and still remains, the ideal and pattern beyond all rules and statutes. He himself became conscious of this to the point that he had to make it clear at times that what he demanded of himself he could not expect of others.[51]

Early Franciscanism then was to a very large degree the adoption of the life of Francis — a perceived means to a greater and higher degree of Christian perfection. Saint Francis was convinced that he had had a divinely inspired insight into a more perfect way of following Christ and it was his desire to follow out that insight in the very way he led his life. It was for him a new way and he made a conscious break with the older and more established institutional forms that then existed for the pursuit of Christian perfection: "I would that you name not me any other rule, whether that of Saint Augustine, or that of Saint Benedict, or that of Saint Bernard" the *Speculum Perfectionis* has him say.[52]

Basically, Francis wanted to imitate the Christ of the Gospels as perfectly as he could; to ascend mystically into a complete union with Him. That others saw the real possibility of following Christ in the life of Francis explains the origins of the Franciscan *religio*. This is an important fact to keep in mind because it helps both to understand why the prose writings occur almost without exception in the latter part of his life in such an occasional manner and as almost peripheral to his career and also why it is possible to see certain common threads running through these writings, disparate as they are. Indeed, I feel that a close analysis of the prose writings shows a certain conceptual unity.

The prose works were mostly (if not entirely) written after 1220 and they reflect both the growth of the order and the inevitable problems connected with that growth. The *Rules* were necessary to satisfy the exigencies of canon law and to outline the minimal standards and demands of the Franciscan way of life. The *Testaments* must be read in conjunction with the evolution of the *Rules* and must be seen, at least partially, as an attempt on the part of Francis to keep the pristine spirit of the order from erosion. The *Admonitions* and the *Letters* must be seen as part of the larger preaching mission of the saint and as a part of his total apostolic ministry of preaching. In short, the writings, taken as a group, had a certain unity of purpose: to further the ideals of the Franciscan conception of perfection through internal reform and exterior propaganda.

The essence of the Franciscan religious message was at the same time deceptively simple and quite complex. It had great, almost total, originality and yet was rooted in a much larger and older Christian ascesis. The religious mysticism of Saint Francis owed very little to that strain of religious ascesis called *theologia negativa*. His spiritual forebearers were not the neo-Platonists or the Pseudo-Dionysius. He did not attempt to deny the senses in any radical way or turn his back on the material. It is not easy, for example, to compare the mysticism of Francis with Meister Eckhart or even John of the Cross. On the contrary, Saint Francis belonged to that tradition of Christian mysticism that had as its ancestors Origen in the Patristic period and Saint Bernard of Clairvaux in the early medieval era. It was a Christ-centered mysticism and is summed up in a sentence from Thomas of Celano (*Second Life*): "*Tota in Christum suum anima sitiebat; totum illi non solum cordis sed corporis dedicabat.*" (His whole soul thirsted for Christ and he dedicated to him his body as well as his heart.)[53]

This following of Christ is a leitmotiv that runs throughout all the prose writings of Francis. It was not simply that Christ was some sort of ethical paradigm to be used as a practical model for behavior but that Saint Francis totally believed that Christ was God in the flesh (the *theanthropos* of Origen). This was the absolutely crucial basis for all of the religious activity of Saint Francis; in the very first *Admonition* Francis states that anyone who fails to see and believe that "He is the true Son of God is damned" and in the long exhortation to the friars which makes up cap. 22 of the *Rule of 1221* Francis says simply that the friars as a basis for their lives "must hold fast to the words, the life, the teachings, and the holy gospel of Our Lord Jesus Christ."

The core belief of Saint Francis in the centrality of the Incarnation is the basis for the other themes that run through the writings. It explains, for example, the continued emphasis in the prose works on the Holy Eucharist. We have already noted that the subject of the Eucharist is in the *Admonitions* and the *Testament* and forms almost the sole subject matter of the *Letter to All the Faithful*, the *Letter to All Clerics*, and the *Letter to All Superiors*. Saint Francis provides us in the writings with a linkup between the doctrine of the Incarnation and the Holy Eucharist; for him devotion to the Eucharist and the exaltation of that belief merely spells out the profound implications of the Incarnation itself. The humility and the "hiddenness" of Christ in the Incarnation are qualities that are continued in time and history through the Eucharist; as he notes in that key passage of the *Admonition*: "Every day He comes to us and lets us see Him in abjection, when He descends from the bosom of the Father into the hands of the priest at the altar. He shows Himself to us in this sacred bread just as He once appeared to His apostles in real flesh."

As corollaries to this continued fascination with the reality of Christ both in the Incarnation and in the Holy Eucharist are the other ways in which Christ is made real to the eyes of the believer.

These corollaries run like threads through the whole tapestry of the prose corpus. The humility of Christ and His "hiddenness" is best understood in the most humble events of His life, especially in His nativity and in His passion and death on the cross. Francis had a strong and intense devotion to the Blessed Virgin because she was the earthly instrument for the Incarnation. He had a profound and sacramental devotion to the Scriptures because the humble written word revealed the life and the glory of Christ.

One theme in the life of Francis that receives a good deal of attention in the legends and is picked up in art is noticeably lacking in the prose writings: his love for nature and the creatures of the world. This may be a bit surprising at first but only if we have totally accepted the romantic figure of Saint Francis which has been nurtured by the romantic rediscovery of the saint in the last century. Unfortunately, those who began to reappreciate the life of the saint in that period tended to detach his love for nature from his religious orientation so that his love for nature began to be sentimentalized; the tendency was to read Francis not against the background of the Gospels and Christian spirituality but against the background of Wordsworth and the Romantics. It will be argued later in this book (and especially in connection with the *Canticle of Brother Sun*) that one cannot really understand the Franciscan love for nature in a manner detached from his more mainline christological concerns and his sacramental view of the world based on his acceptance of the world as a created gift from God.

The prose writings of Saint Francis are not easy to read. They reflect a world and a *zeitgest* that is foreign to all but the most keenly tuned religious sensibility. Yet for all their seemingly foreign style they are important, if not fundamental, documents in the history of Christian religious thought. They manifest and testify to a new and important shift in religious spirituality. The higher synthesis of Christocentric mysticism, shown both in the writings of the saint and in his life, enriched not only the whole history of religion in the West but added new possibilities for the sensibility of Western religious art; the prose writings provided the background for that "April freshness that is Giotto," to use John Ruskin's memorable phrase. In the field of spirituality the dominant themes of the mystical theology of Saint Francis of Assisi were pursued and deepened by a whole line of saints and scholars who followed in the Franciscan tradition: Saint Anthony of Padua, Saint Bonaventure, John Duns Scotus, Blessed Angela of Foligno, and San Bernardino of Siena.

CHAPTER 2

The Prayers and the Poetry

B ESIDES the prose writings of Saint Francis, there are a series of prayers that have been satisfactorily attributed to his pen. These prayers fall into three classes: the *Praises* which he wrote in Latin, the *Liturgical Office of the Passion,* and the vernacular canticle-poem *The Canticle of Brother Sun.* These writings date from various times in the life of Francis but, with the exception of the *Praises of the Most High* and the *Canticle of Brother Sun* which can be dated to the last years of his life, it is impossible to put the other prayers into any accurate chronology.

The prayers of Francis are far more interesting to the student of literature than are the prose writings. They reflect a style of writing and a devotional method that encouraged the development of the so-called Laudist tradition in Italy which culminated in the poetry of Jacopone da Todi, one of the greatest of the *Trecento* Italian poets. In this chapter we will not only discuss in some depth the poetic compositions of Francis but also the way in which these prayers encouraged the development of the tradition of the *lauda.*

I *The Latin* Laudes *(Praises) of Saint Francis*

There is conserved in a reliquary at the Basilica of Saint Francis in Assisi a sheet of paper which contains on one side a prayer, written in the hand of the saint, and on the opposite side, again in the hand of the saint, the Aaronic blessing ("The Lord bless thee and keep thee/The Lord turn his countenance to thee and give thee peace" Numbers 6: 24 - 26) and the added emphatic blessing "May God bless you, Brother Leo." Between the letters E and O of LEO Francis also drew a Greek cross (similar to the Greek letter *Tau*) with what appears to be a head or a skull under the cross. Underneath this blessing, in another hand, is noted: "Blessed Francis wrote this

blessing with his own hand for me, Brother Leo." At the very bottom
of the page is noted: "In like manner he made this sign Tau together
with the head in his own hand." The head — not clearly legible on
the parchment — may make reference to Calvary (the place of the
skull; Latin: *calvus* — bald) and the cross. The ensemble would then
refer both to the Passion of Christ and to the stigmata of Francis on
Mount La Verna.

Two sources explain the origin of this document and tell us about
the composition of the prayer which is now known as the *Praises of
the Most High* or the *Praises of God* which is written on the opposite
side from the *Blessing of Brother Leo*. The first is the Assisi
autograph itself. On the side of the parchment which contains the
Blessing of Brother Leo a rather long notation says that two years
before the death of the saint, while making a retreat from August
through September on Mount La Verna, Francis had a vision of the
Lord, after which he received the impressions of the wounds of
Christ on his own body (i.e., the stigmatization) and "after the vision
and the speech of the Seraph and the impression of the stigmata of
Christ in his body, he made and wrote with his own hand the *Praises*
written on the other side of this sheet, giving thanks to the Lord for
the benefits conferred upon him."

The second account of this incident, which really fleshes out the
one we have quoted above from the autograph itself, is found in
Thomas of Celano's *Second Life* of the saint. In this account Brother
Leo asks Saint Francis for something to help him overcome a
spiritual temptation while they are together on Mount La Verna. In
answer to that request, Saint Francis called for paper and wrote
down the praises upon which he had himself been meditating during
the time of the retreat: "He wrote down with his own hand the
Praises of God and the words he wanted and lastly a blessing for that
brother saying 'Take this paper and guard it carefully till the day of
your death.' "[1] Evidently Brother Leo followed the injunction quite
scrupulously since the conserved parchment is largely unintelligible
except to paleographers, at least on the side on which the *Praises of
God* are written, due to repeated foldings of the parchment, handling, and use. Indeed, most scholars have turned to early
manuscript texts of the *Praises of God* to get the best reading (due to
the obscurities in the autograph itself caused by the wear and tear on
it).

The *Praises of God* that Saint Francis composed are these:

You alone are holy, Lord God, Worker of Wonders
You are strong
You are great
You are the Most High
You are omnipotent, our Holy Father, Lord of Heaven and Earth
You, Lord God, one and three, are our every good
You Lord God, are good, all good, our highest good, our highest good —
Lord God

                                                    Living and True
You are charity and love
You are wisdom
You are humility
You are patience
You are a firm anchor
You are peace
You are joy and happiness
You are justice and temperance
You are fulness of riches
You are beauty
You are gentleness
You are our protector
You are our guardian and defender
You are our strength
You are our great hope
You are our faith
You are our most profound sweetness
You are our Eternal Life, great and admirable Lord, Omnipotent God
                              Holy and Merciful Saviour.[2]

When one looks at the text of this prayer (which is reproduced in
its entirety above) certain things become immediately evident. First,
the simple and evocative style of this prayer stands in sharp contrast
to the more prosaic and flat style of the prose that we considered in
an earlier chapter. The only thing in the prose copies that is remotely
like this is the twenty-seventh *Admonition* which is written in a
somewhat similar style. Secondly, it is quite easy to see how this
prayer gets the title of a laud since it does not include any of the
other traditional modes of prayer in it (e.g., petition, petition for
forgiveness, a form of penance, thanksgiving) but is a pure hymn of
praise rather similar to both psalms of praise from the Bible and certain liturgical usages. This is an important point since this links the
prayer firmly in the tradition of the laud and, as such, must be seen
in somewhat the same light as the *Canticle of Brother Sun.* These
lauds added immensely to the whole tradition of the *laudisti* who

had their origin in the years just before the saint's death, a tradition that swept over Italy after the death of the saint, largely under the influence of the Franciscans.

Stylistically the prayer is quite simple, taking its origin probably from the short invocations that Francis would have been familiar with both from the official liturgy of the time and from extra-liturgical sources. The short declamations litanize honorific titles of God, titles which are either taken directly from biblical sources or paraphrases from that same tradition. The Book of Psalms was evidently an abundant source for the prayer of Francis with its descriptions of God as just, strong, defender, source of hope, etc.

We have no clear evidence from the early Franciscan sources as to how, and under what conditions, this prayer was used. It is not improbable that it was used both in private devotions and also sung either by an individual or chorally. As we shall see later in this chapter, the singing of prayers and impromptu hymns was not only common practice for Francis and the early friars but was characteristic of their spirituality and their method of evangelization.

Besides the *Praises of God* Francis also composed another laud-prayer which is called the *Praise of the Virtues*. Again, we do not know when or under what circumstances Francis wrote this prayer but it is attested to in the earliest manuscripts and is alluded to in Celano's *Second Life* of the saint.[3]

The *Praises of the Virtues* is composed of logically distinguishable parts. The first section of the *Praises* exalts six virtues: Regal Wisdom and her sister Simplicity; Lady Poverty and her sister Humility; Lady Love with her sister Obedience. The next section of the *Praise* has some didactic lines which teach that a person cannot possess any of the virtues without "dying to self" and if one possesses a single virtue, not offending against the others, that person "possesses all," and vice versa. The final strophes then indicate how the virtues that are praised in the laud can put vice to flight: Holy Wisdom overcomes Satan, Poverty routs greed and avarice, Simplicity overshadows the wisdom of this world, etc. The last lines of the *Praise of the Virtues* then single out Obedience as the virtue that chastises the body, keeps people submissive, and pliable to the will of God. Here is the complete text of the *Praise of the Virtues:*

I salute you, Regal Wisdom. May the Lord safeguard you with your holy sister, Unsullied Simplicity.
Holy Lady Poverty! May the Lord watch over you and your sister, Holy Humility.

My pious Lady Charity! May the Lord watch over you and your holy sister,
Obedience.
May the Lord protect all of you holy virtues, for you found your55source in
Him and come forth from Him.
No man in this world can possess you if he does not die to self.
He who possesses one of you, without offending the others, possesses all.
He who offends one of you lacks all and offends against all.
Each of you drives out vice and sin.
Holy Wisdom overcomes Satan and his wiles.
Holy and pure Simplicity confounds the wisdom of this world and fleshly
desires.
Holy Poverty drives out cupidity, avarice, and earthly desire.
Holy Humility overcomes pride, the men of this world, and all terrestrial
things.
Holy Charity confounds all temptations of the flesh and the devil and all
human fears.
Holy Obedience drives out carnal and bodily desires and keeps the body in
check.
It holds us subject to the Spirit and obedient to our brothers.
It keeps us submissive to all the men of the world, and not only to men, but
to the animals and to the flowers, who can do what they want with us to the
extent that God has given them power over us.[4]

The *Praise of the Virtues*, while in the tradition of the laud, has
significant differences when compared with the *Praises of the Most
High*. The latter is quite straightforward, without any trace of the
didactic, and with a far more universal appeal. It seems evident,
judging from the strong plea for obedience that one finds in the final
lines of the *Praises of the Virtues*, that this particular prayer was
directed to the more limited audience of the friars themselves. It also
might give us reason to date this prayer from after 1220 when the
question of obedience became more acute within the Franciscan
order. Its strong didactic element also makes it more plausible to
think of it less as a song of praise and more as a strophic sermon.

For all the criticism that one can make of the *Praise of the Virtues*
it does have the one strong Franciscan trait of characterizing the virtues in familiar and relational terms: Lady Poverty, Sister Humility,
etc. This is something that Francis made his very own and carried to
supreme poetical heights in the *Canticle of Brother Sun*. It forms
part of the very core of Franciscan humanism. Francis not only
called the dumb creatures of this world by the title of "brother" or
"sister" but extended this appellation to the virtues and even to
those things that men hate and abhor: when Francis was to have his

eyes cauterized with a white-hot iron (a medical remedy of the time) he said to the iron, "Brother Fire, I pray you be courteous with me"; and during his last hours he cried out a greeting to "Sister Death." The *Praises of the Virtues* give eloquence to this basic part of the Franciscan tradition of humanism.

It should be noted also that in the very last part of the section on Holy Obedience, the text insists that obedience be rendered, not only to God and to the brethren, but also to animals and flowers. It is impossible, given the state of studies on Franciscan chronology, to know if this prayer was written before or after the *Canticle of Brother Sun* (my own position is that it was probably written shortly before, perhaps a year or so before) but, apart from the *Canticle*, this is the one time in the writings of the saint where he gives substance to an idea that appears so often in the *Legends*: the relationship of nature and spirituality. It is only a passing reference in this prayer but does underscore an important point, a point that will be emphasized later in this chapter. Francis did not relate to the natural world from a purely naturalistic frame of reference. It is a mistake to place him in the category of a Richard Jeffries or even a William Wordsworth. As this small reference shows, Francis saw men not as being overawed by nature but as part of the whole universe. He did not emphasize the mastery of man over the world but man as part of the total cosmos and obedient to the inherent laws in that cosmos and responsible to those laws even to the point where he is subordinate (i.e., obedient) to the place of animals and plants who also share in the rightness of being as part of the totality of creation.

In many of the earliest manuscripts of the *Praises of the Virtues* there is appended a concluding laud in honor of the Blessed Virgin Mary; other manuscripts preserve this *Salutation of the Blessed Virgin* (as it is most commonly called) as a separate and distinct prayer. It is difficult to know if at one time these two prayers went together or not, but today they are usually printed and listed as distinct prayers. This probably is a better practice since Thomas of Celano tells us that Francis "sang special praises to her [the Virgin], poured out prayers to her, offered her his affections, so many and so great that the tongue cannot recount them."[5] This would seem to indicate that Francis wrote quite separate lauds in the Virgin's honor.

The *Salutation* begins with a salute to our "Holy Lady/Most Holy Queen/and Mother of God." Then her relation to the Holy Trinity is recounted: Mary is chosen by the Father, consecrated by the Father and the Son, and the recipient of the Holy Spirit. The next section of the *Salutation* litanizes some of the titles of the Virgin; she is a palace (i.e., the dwelling place of the royal Jesus), a tabernacle, a robe, a handmaiden (cf. Luke 1: 38), and mother. The *Salutation* then concludes with another praise of all the virtues which are poured out into the hearts of men so that they are "faithless no longer." The complete text of the *Salutation* reads:

Mary, I salute you. You are our Holy Lady, Most Holy Queen, and Mother of God.
You are ever Virgin, elect of the Father, consecrated by Him with His most holy beloved Son and the Holy Paraclete.
In you is the fullness of grace and all good.
I salute you as the palace, tabernacle, and house of God.
I salute you, His garment;
                    His handmaid;
                    His mother.[6]

This laud in honor of the Virgin is somewhat similar to the *Praises of the Most High* in that both prayers have, as their central motif, the listing of honorifics that are meant to magnify the virtue and the glory of the one addressed. In terms of their genre these lauds belong to a tradition of litanies, lauds, and eulogies that can be traced back to the early Middle Ages (one litany of the Virgin in Gaelic can be dated to the eighth century) but reached their fullest flower in the twelfth century. These are litanies for private or nonliturgical use; the liturgical litanies (e.g., the *Kyrie Eleison)* have a much older history. The many litanies and lauds that were common all through the Middle Ages were finally stabilized and recognized as authentic works of piety in the sixteenth century when such litanies as the *Litany of Loreto* (in honor of the Virgin) and the *Litany of All the Saints* were recognized for universal use by the Catholic faithful.[7] In that sense, Francis was utilizing a genre that was not original with him and one that was to have a long history after his time. What distinguishes these particular lauds is what Matthew Arnold called the "limpid mysticism of them that never turns fanatic" and the influence that they, along with the *Canticle of Brother Sun,* have had on the whole tradition of the *lauda* in Italian literature, a topic to be discussed later in this chapter.

There is one other laud that can be attributed to the pen of Saint Francis. In the oldest manuscript that we have cataloging the writings of the saint (Assisi 338), a notation reads: "Here begins the praises which our blessed father Francis arranged and recited at every Hour of the day and night and before the Office of the Blessed Virgin Mary." Under that notation is a laud that was composed for recitation before the Hours of the Office.

This laud consists of six passages taken from Holy Scripture (five passages from the Book of Revelation and one from the Book of Daniel) with the corresponding response, "Let us praise and glorify Him forever." The doxology is then added (Glory be to the Father/and to the Son/and to the Holy Ghost/etc.) with the same response; the laud then concludes with a prayer that is a prose paraphrase of the response "Let us praise and glorify him forever." A sample verse will give an adequate idea of the style of this *Praise before the Office:*

> "Thou art worthy, O Lord Our God,
> To receive glory, honor, and power" (cf. Rev. 4:11)
> R. "Let us praise and glorify Him forever."

The structure of this laud and, indeed, its very title, indicates that Saint Francis wrote it as a preliminary praise of God to be used by the friars as they began the choral recitation of the Canonical Hours. This laud (and the *Office of the Passion* which Francis also composed) illustrates the lack of absolute uniformity in the canonical usages of this period. It was not until the Council of Trent in the sixteenth century that such particular additions to the liturgy were outlawed. There is no particular originality in this laud but it does illustrate once again the ample use of Scripture that Francis employed in his compositions and thus reminds us to look for biblical analogues in the writings of the saint.[8]

II *The* Office of the Passion

The *Office of the Passion* belongs among the writings of Saint Francis only in the sense that he arranged the scriptural verses of this supplemental breviary for his friars and added a few words of his own throughout the text. The *Office of the Passion* is modelled on the larger Office which was the public prayer of the Church said in choir by monks, nuns, and cathedral chapters in all the Christian world at stated intervals during the day and night. Saint Francis was not the only one to compose a parallel office; right down to modern times there have been shorter versions of the office used with some frequency by religious communities or privately by pious persons, the *Office of the Virgin,* the *Office of the Dead,* and the very popular "Short Breviary," being just a few examples of this modified liturgical usage.

The *Office of the Passion* which Saint Francis arranged was composed to extend over the whole cycle of the liturgical year and was divided into five parts:

1) An Office for the last two days of Holy Week which would begin at Compline (night prayers) of Holy Thursday. This section then would also be used on ordinary days of the week for the rest of the year.
2) A different set of psalms and prayers for the Easter season.
3) Another cycle for the Sundays and principal feasts of the year.
4) An Advent cycle (the four weeks prior to Christmas).
5) A Christmas cycle.

Each of the Hours of the Office (Compline/Matins/Prime/Tierce/Sext/None/Vespers) would consist of an antiphon (an introductory verse), "Holy Virgin Mary," and then a psalm. The psalms that Saint Francis used were not taken *in toto* from the psalter in the Bible. Francis arranged his own psalms by taking verses, or parts of verses from various places in the Bible and sometimes adding a verse or a line of his own composition; thus a typical line from the *Office of the Passion* might read: "But the Lord redeems the lives of His servants with His own most precious blood/no one incurs guilt who takes refuge in Him."

That line is taken from Psalm 33:23 with the exception of the words "with His own most precious blood" which were added by Saint Francis to emphasize more clearly the christological reading of the psalm. Another example: "Those who repay evil for good harass me for pursuing good/You are my most holy father, my king and my Lord/Make haste to help me, O Lord, my salvation."

In this case the first line is from Psalm 37:21, while the second line is one that Francis composed, and the third line again continues Psalm 37 with verse 23, Francis's line being a substitute for verse twenty-two.[9]

The *Office of the Passion* is not of first-rate importance either in the history of spirituality or in the study of the saint. It has a certain importance as a document in the development of the liturgy and is representative of the more formal aspect of the prayer life of both the saint and the early Franciscans. The practice of this recitation must also be seen in the larger context of the friars' obligation to recite the Office, an obligation that is set down not only in the various *Rules* of the order (cf. cap. # 3 of the *Rule of 1223)* but receives attention both in the *Testament* and, especially, in the *Letter to a General Chapter* where Francis exhorts the friars to sing the Office not with any worry concerning the melodies in themselves but "with their voice in harmony with their mind and their mind in tune with God." From these sources we have a fairly well established liturgical legislation for the early Franciscans: the friars were bound to a recitation of the Office; those who could not read would recite a determined number of *Paters* at the various Hours. The usage of the Office should follow the Roman Breviary but the Psalter used was the old Gallican psalter. Saint Francis saw the Office not only as the official prayer of the Church but also as an exercise in fraternity; thus, as Cajetan Esser has written, the Office "has its full significance only when celebrated in the community of such official prayers. Francis therefore expressly urged that as far as possible all the friars should gather in the oratory and there recite the Office together."[10]

Finally, there is some evidence that Saint Francis extended the use of this *Office of the Passion* outside the confines of his own group of friars. The twentieth chapter of the *Legend of Saint Clare,* written by Thomas of Celano, notes that Clare learned an *Office of the Cross* from Saint Francis who "had composed it and prayed it often with like affection." This *Office of the Cross* has been regarded since the time of Wadding as another title for the *Office of the Passion.* It is worth noting, in this regard, that the *Rule* drawn up for laymen who wished to follow the Franciscan way of life, the so-called "Third Order" (which in its present form does not come from Saint Francis but has him as a remote author), includes a chapter on the Office where clerics are enjoined to recite the Hours "after the manner of the clergy" and instructions for others are given. No mention is made, however, of the Office composed by Saint Francis himself.[11]

III   *The* Canticle of Brother Sun

Saint Francis began to compose the *Canticle of Brother Sun* in 1225, the penultimate year of his life. Despite some scholarly dispute, it is generally accepted that the first part of the *Canticle* (roughly the first twenty-two verses) was written while Francis lay sick at the Poor Clares' convent of San Damiano in Assisi. In fact, a garden is still shown there that is supposed to be the place where he wrote that *Canticle.* The old traditions also say that the saint composed a melody for the *Canticle* at that time and instructed the friars to sing it while they were out on their preaching journey. The second part of the *Canticle* (the verses dealing with reconciliation, peace, and forgiveness) was added by Saint Francis as his way of mediating a dispute that was going on in Assisi between the *podestà* (the mayor) and the local bishop, a dispute that had already resulted in an economic boycott from the civil side and an excommunication from the clerical when Francis intervened. The final verses of the *Canticle*, a salute in honor of "Sister Death," was added by the saint on his deathbed after he had heard his brethren sing the original *Canticle* to him.

The *Canticle of Brother Sun* is written in an Umbrian dialect of Italian and is unrhymed. The poetic structure of the poem is enhanced by the strong assonance and, as is common in Italian, by the repeated use of the soft *l* and *r*. Other instances of this usage in the corpus of the saint's writings are most notably in the Latin *laudes* and, curiously enough, in chapter twenty-one of the *First Rule* (e.g., *timete et honorate/laudate et benedicite/gratias agite et adorate,* etc.) where one can see both the heavily stressed accents of the poetry and the use of the liquid sounds of the language.

It is not hard to detect the direct literary influences on the composition of the *Canticle*. The most obvious sources can be traced to the Bible and, more specifically, to Psalm 148 (Praise ye the Lord from the heavens/praise ye Him in the high places/etc.), the "Canticle of the Three Young Men" in the Book of Daniel (Cap. 3, 52 - 90), some isolated passages from Ecclesiasticus and the Book of Revelations. There is then, in the *Canticle*, as in many of the other writings of the saint, ample evidence of the Bible as an almost automatic source of direct inspiration when Saint Francis put pen to paper. He drew on this material with ease and facility.

While, at first glance, the *Canticle of Brother Sun* is lyrically simple and charmingly direct it is not so easy to understand it fully or to translate it into English due to a *crux* in the wording that presents a formidable problem for the translator. The problem is of such a magnitude that the meaning of the poem largely depends on choices made in the very act of translation. Take the following brief verse from the poem:

Laudato si, Mi Signore, per sora luna e le stelle

The crucial word in that verse is the word *per*. Is the verse to be translated "Be praised, My Lord, through (by means of) sister moon and the stars" or is it to be read "Be praised, My Lord, for (because of) sister moon and the stars."? Both translations make good sense theologically and both can be justified on philological grounds. To make the problem even more vexatious, the thirteenth-century Franciscans who mention the *Canticle* themselves do not always agree in their interpretation of the meaning. Thomas of Celano, in his life of the saint, says that Francis wrote "certain praises of the creatures and incited them to praise the Creator," while the unknown author of the *Speculum Perfectionis* (which reflects a very ancient tradition based on the testimony of close companions of the saint) insists that Francis wrote the *Canticle* to incite men to praise God for all the goodness that He had bestowed on men and for all of the good gifts that He had granted them.[12]

When the *Canticle* is compared to the other writings of the saint still no light is shed on the matter. In the *Letter to all the Faithful* Francis exhorts all creatures to render praises to God (adopting this idea from Revelations 5 : 13 and Psalm 148, both of which texts had an influence on the *Canticle)* while in the *First Rule of 1221* (cap. xxiii) Francis exhorts every creature to render thanksgiving to God. In short, both the idea of cosmic praise and constant thanksgiving occur in the writings of the saint.[13]

One modern biographer of Saint Francis, insisting that neither translation can be proven to be the exact one, threw all poetry to the wind and simply translated the *per* verses (there are nine of them) in English showing both usages: "Be praised, My Lord by/for Sister moon and the stars."[14] In my own published translation of the *Canticle* I used *per* for while aware that it was only one possibility from which to choose.[15] It is quite possible that the *per* can mean both thanksgiving and praise at the same time and that it is simply impossible to translate that dual sense in English. My own inclination is to admit that double sense in light of the different readings that were given to the *Canticle* in the time of Francis himself.

The *Canticle* begins with an opening praise of the "Bon Signore" who is most high and about whom no person is really worthy to speak. The poet then adds that the Creator is to be praised together with all His creation *(con tutte le sue creature)* especially Brother Sun who reminds us so much of God Himself *(de te, Altissimo, porta significazione).* There follows then a series of praises in which the elements of the cosmos, the earth, and Mother earth herself is called on to praise *(per-*through) or for which the Lord is praised *(per-*for) as the giver of these things:

Be praised, My Lord, for our sister water/
useful and humble, precious and clear.

Be praised, My Lord, for our brother fire/
through whom light comes in darkness/
He is bright and pleasant, mighty and robust.

The next section of the *Canticle* praises those who pardon for the love of God and accept tribulation; those who accept and cultivate such peace will be crowned in heaven *(sirano incoronati)*. These are the four verses that Francis added during the civil strife in Assisi as a conciliatory sermon to his own warring townfolks.

The next six lines of the *Canticle* were added when Francis lay dying. The Lord is praised by/for "our sister bodily death" *(sora nostra morte corporale)* whom no man can escape. The true woe is reserved for those who die in sin, but those who die in the grace of God will not see the "second death" *(la seconda morte,* i.e., eternal damnation). The canticle then concludes: Praise and Bless My Lord/Thank and Serve Him with great humility.

The *Canticle of Brother Sun* has been the best known and the most appreciated of all the written works of the saint. It was the one literary work of the Italian *Duecento* that most captured the imagination of the nineteenth-century critic and played a significant role in the rediscovery of the beauty of the medieval world that started at that time.[16] We have already seen that Francis had been characterized as a lay rebel against the clericalized church of the Middle Ages; similarly there is a somewhat distorted picture of Francis (coming largely from this poem and a few of the nature stories) as a near-pantheistic nature mystic. It was the tendency of the nineteenth-century critic (and one still runs across this characterization today) to see Francis as a charmingly pastoral and bucolic *naïf* in love with the beauties of the Umbrian countryside. That Francis loved the natural world is undeniable; that he was a "nature mystic" is, at the very least, a distortion.

At one level the *Canticle of Brother Sun* is a supremely orthodox and medieval poem. Its debt to the canticles and praises of the Bible (and to liturgical sources) is quite clear. Even setting aside the very real problem of how to translate the poem in the *per* passages, the intention of the poem is quite obvious. The *Canticle* does not evidence any type of "nature religion" if one means by that phrase anything similar to the thought of Richard Jeffries or William Wordsworth.

When Saint Francis looked at the world around him and saw evidences of the Creator in that world he was only giving credence to a tradition in the Christian world that was common in his own time and went back at least to the time of John Scotus Erigena in the ninth century: God is revealed to men by means of two books: the Bible and the world of nature.[17] This was axiomatic in the medieval world and it was the basis both of all medieval iconography and whatever natural science there was.

Francis did not make a rather unique addition to this medieval notion that the world was to be thought of as God's encyclopedia. Francis thought of all of creation as living in a spirit of fraternity and community. Professor Lynn White, Jr. has called Francis the greatest radical in the history of Christianity because of this "democratic spirit": "Francis tried to depose man from his monarchy over creation and set up a democracy of all creatures. With him the ant is no longer simply a homily for the lazy, flames a sign of the thrust of the soul towards union with God; now they are Brother Ant and Sister Fire, praising the Creator in their own way as Brother Man does in his way."[18]

The *Canticle of Brother Sun* must be read against the whole background of the stories of Francis preaching to the birds, exhorting the flowers in the field to praise God, redeeming lambs being taken to the slaughterhouse, taming the wolf of Gubbio, insisting that his friars cut wood in the forest in such a way as to let the trees live. In that whole attitude toward the natural world there was a profound awareness of the utter goodness of God's creation (an insight basic to the creation of myth in the Book of Genesis) and the total dependence of all of creation, including man, on the providence of God. It would be a mistake to see this attitude as pantheism. One reads both the *Canticle* and the nature stories with the clear perception that Francis was keenly aware of the separation between Creator and creatures. As if to emphasize this distance Francis completed the *Canticle* with the injunction that the world of creation is both to thank *(rengraziate)* the Lord and "serve Him with great humility" *(serviteli cun grande umilitate)*. In fact, it is interesting to note that Saint Francis never uses the word nature to refer to the world. His perception of the world was much more specified. In his brilliantly perceptive, albeit eccentric, life of the saint, Gilbert K. Chesterton has understood this better than most:

This is the quality in which, as a poet, he is the very opposite of the pantheist. He did not call nature his mother; he called a particular donkey his brother or a particular sparrow his sister . . . Saint Francis was a mystic, but he believed in mysticism not mystification. As a mystic he was the mortal enemy of those mystics who melt away the edges of things and dissolve an entity into its environment. He was a mystic of the daylight and the darkness; but not a mystic of the twilight. He was the very contrary of that sort of oriental visionary who is only a mystic because he is too much of a skeptic to be a materialist.[19]

In sum, the *Canticle of Brother Sun* is the poetic *credo* of the medieval belief in the beauty, goodness, and intelligibility of the created world. It sums up that tradition that can be seen in the hymns, the arts, and the poetry of the period. It was a tradition of wonder and of thanksgiving in front of the world that existed after Saint Francis and one that still could be found in the time of Shakespeare.[20] Under the impact of late Renaissance science and the Enlightenment it lost its eminence and was replaced by a sense of marvel at the orderliness of the world. But this Newtonian world view would also go by the boards as the world became secularized and relativized in our post-Einsteinian period. The *Canticle* testifies to a simpler time and, as such, still creates a sense of nostalgia and loss at our half-forgotten innocence.

The *Canticle of Brother Sun* can lay legitimate claim to an important and lasting place in the history of the literature of the Western world. It can make that claim not only in terms of its importance for the beginnings of Italian poetry but also because of the continued fascination that it has had for students and lovers of literature. But, in the final analysis, one must agree with the measured judgment of Giovanni Getto, that the *Canticle of Brother Sun* was born "not as a poetic gesture but as an act of religion." It must be considered, not as an independent entity to be inserted at will in an anthology of Italian poetry, but in terms of the rich liturgical background from which it sprung and only against which is it totally intelligible. It is only understandable in terms of the scriptural soil that nourished it and scriptural tradition that inspired it. Seen in this light, and keeping firmly in mind the whole medieval traditional theology of the creative work of God, one can view the canticle both in terms of its traditional *locus* and its startling originality, an originality that is seen not only in the vigor of its language but in the spontaneity of its lyrical mysticism. If my insistence on repeating over again in this section the traditional source and theology of the *Canticle of Brother*

Sun seems a bit excessive it is not because of sheer redundancy; it is because of the firm conviction that the only way to focus on the originality of the saint and his work is to resist the impulse to romanticize him into something that he is not. The real genius of Saint Francis was that he was able to be so fully a part of the whole tradition of thirteenth-century Christian Europe while, at the same time, transcending and redoing some elements of that culture. Saint Francis was a man of the Middle Ages and nourished himself on the wisdom of that era. What vaulted him into historical prominence was his creative ability to show forth new forces at work in that ancient culture.

Because of the fundamental importance of the *Canticle of Brother Sun* in the corpus of his writings, I reproduce the text of the Italian version below with my own English translation:

> Altissimo omnipotente bon signore
> tue so le laude la gloria e l'onore e omne benedizione.
>
> A te solo, Altissimo, se confano
> e null omo e digno te montovare.
>
> Laudato sie, mi Signore, cun tutte le tue creature,
> spetialmente messer lo frate sole
> lo qual e iorno et allumini noi per loi
>
> Et ellu e bellu e radiante cum grande splendore
> da te, Altissimo, porta significatione.
>
> Laudato si', mi Signore, per sora luna e le stelle
> il celu l'ai formate clarite et pretiose et belle.
>
> Laudato si', mi signore, per frate vento
> et per aere et nubilo et sereno et onne tempo
> per lo quale a le tue creature dai sustentamento.
>
> Laudato si', mi Signore, per sor acqua,
> la quale e multo utile et humile et pretiosa et casta.
>
> Laudato si', mi Signore, per frate focu,
> per lo quale ennallumini la nocte
> ed e bello et iocundo et robustoso et forte.

Laudato si', mi Signore, per sora nostra matre terra
la quale ne sustenta et governa
et produce diversi fructi con coloriti fiori et herba.

Laudato si, mi Signore, per quelli le perdonano per lo tuo amore
et sostengo infirmitate et tribulatione
beati quelli kel sosterano in pace
ka da te, Altissimo, sirano incoronati.

Laudato si', mi Signore, per sora mostra morte corporale
da la quale nullo homo vivente po skappare
quai acquelli ke morrano ne le peccata mortali

Beati quelli ke trovara ne le tue sanctissime voluntati
ka la morte secunda nol farra male.

Laudate et benedicite mi'Signore et rengratiate
et serviateli cum grande humiliatate.[21]

Most High, omnipotent, good Lord
To you alone belong praise and glory,
Honor and blessing.
No man is worthy to breathe thy name.

Be praised, my Lord, for all your creatures.
In the first place for the blessed Brother Sun,
who gives us the day and enlightens us through you.
He is beautiful and radiant with great splendor,
Giving witness of thee, Most Omnipotent One.

Be praised, my Lord, for Sister Moon and the stars
Formed by you so bright, precious, and beautiful.

Be praised, my Lord, for Brother Wind
And the airy skies, so cloudy and serene;
For every weather, be praised, for it is life-giving.

Be praised, my Lord, for Sister Water,
So necessary, yet so humble and precious, and chaste.

Be praised, my Lord, for Brother Fire,
Who lights up the night.
He is beautiful and carefree, robust and fierce.

Be praised, my Lord, for our sister, Mother Earth,
Who nourishes and watches us
While bringing forth abundance of fruits with colored flowers
and herbs.

Be praised, my Lord, for those who pardon through your love
And bear weakness and trial,
Blessed are those who endure in peace,
For they will be crowned by you, Most High.

Be praised, my Lord, for our sister, Bodily Death,
Whom no living man can escape.
Woe to those who die in sin.
Blessed are those who discover thy holy will.
The second death will do them no harm.

Praise and bless my Lord.
Render thanks.
Serve him with great humility.

                                   Amen.[22]

IV   *The Poetic Influence of Saint Francis*

Up to this point we have disussed the various lauds and poems
that Saint Francis wrote both in Italian and in Latin. It is most important to remember that these prayers and lauds were not written
specifically to be read in prayerbooks but were to be sung either by
the friars as part of their preaching exercises or as a part of their own
devotions. Even though we have only a mere handful of lauds from
the pen of Francis abundant evidence in the early sources indicates
that he wrote other hymns and songs that have not come down to us.
Indeed, there are numerous recollections in the early *Lives* of the
saint of his spontaneously breaking into an improvised song. We
know also that Saint Francis not only composed the *Canticle of
Brother Sun* but also composed a now lost melody for it. He ordered
his brethren to sing it while they were on their preaching journeys
and he had it sung to him when he was on his own deathbed; after
the performance he added the verses about the welcome of "Sister
Death."

More significantly, the sources tell us that when Francis broke out
into spontaneous song he often did that singing in French rather
than in Italian or Latin. Thus, in the *Legenda Major* of Saint
Bonaventure Francis is depicted as walking through a forest while

singing the praises of God in French (*laudes Domino lingua Francorum Vir Dei decantaret*).[23] *The Legend of the Three Companions* tells of Francis and some of his companions travelling on foot through the Marches of Ancona with "Francis in a loud clear voice singing praises to God in French."'[24] There is also this charming description of the saint in the *Second Life* of Thomas of Celano: "At times, as we saw with our own eyes, he would pick up a stick from the ground and putting it over his left arm, would draw across it, as across a violin, a little bow bent with a string, and going through the motions of playing, he would sing in French about his Lord."[25]

This familiarity and preference for the French language must also be seen against the broader background of the fondness of Francis for metaphors, analogies, and techniques taken from the French tradition of the troubadour and jongleur which by that time had penetrated all through Italy.[26] Francis likened his followers to the knights of Charlemagne and Roland. He once referred to one of his early companions, Fra Egidio, as a "knight of the round table" (*iste est miles tabulae rotundae*).[27] Perhaps the best-known use of the chivalric tradition is to be found in Francis's interpretation of the knight's lady. Francis, like any true knight, pledged his love and fidelity to a chosen lady: Lady Poverty. In the *Legend of The Three Companions* he answered a query as to whether he had chosen a lady with the answer that he had chosen a lady (i.e., Lady Poverty) "more noble, endowed, and beautiful" than the questioner had ever imagined and, furthermore, he was of a mind to wed her.[28] That incident occurred in his youth; in his last days, he gave, as a part of the *Short Testament*, the injunction that his followers should love and cherish Lady Poverty.

The peculiar *gestalt* that results from the blending of the jongleur singing of the courtly tradition that had come out of France into Italy (and which had influenced Francis so much) with a simple presentation of the truths of the Gospel is a blend characteristically Franciscan. The tradition did not die with Saint Francis for, as Edward Hutton has said, "Saint Francis set the world singing."[29] The early friars were long to remember that Saint Francis had commanded them to go out into the world and become "minstrels for the Lord" (*joculatores Domini*):

He said that he would like the friar who was the best preacher to speak to the people first and afterwards they were all to sing the *Praises of the Lord* together as ministrels of God. And having finished the *Praises* the preacher was to say to the people 'We are God's ministrels, and ask you to repay us for our songs by living in true repentance.'[30]

One way in which the tradition of song poetry, initiated by Saint Francis, was continued in the Franciscan Order after his death was in the outpouring of hymns, songs, and metrical poems that came from the pens of Franciscans both in Italy and in other countries. Much of this poetry which has survived is only of antiquarian interest but some of it has not only survived but until very recently was part of the living tradition of Catholic worship.[31] Thus Thomas of Celano, the first official biographer of the saint, is generally accepted as the author of one of the greatest of medieval hymns, the *Dies Irae*; Jacopone da Todi (who will be discusssed later in this chapter) is possibly the author of the *Stabat Mater Dolorosa*.[32]

The *Dies Irae* of Thomas of Celano is a long metrical poem written in tercets (*Dies irae, dies illa/solvet saeclum in favilla/teste David cum sybila*, etc.) on the theme of judgment and death. It was not originally written for the official liturgy of the Roman Church but soon found its way into the Mass for the Dead and was sung at every Catholic funeral until the liturgical reform after the Second Vatican Council in the late 1960s.

The *Stabat Mater* of Jacopone da Todi is a hymn in honor of Christ's Passion addressed to the Virgin as she stands at the foot of the Cross. It strongly emphasizes the human sufferings of Christ and the empathetic sufferings of the Virgin in the drama of Calvary — themes close to the Franciscan ethos:

> At the Cross her station keeping,
> Stood the Sorrowful Mother weeping
> While on the Cross her Son did hang
> (*Stabat Mater dolorosa/*
> *juxta crucem lacrimonosa/*
> *dum pendebat Filius*)

The *Stabat Mater* of Jacopone da Todi is closely identified with the services of Good Friday in the Roman Catholic Church and is a hymn commonly sung, often in translation, during the paraliturgical services of the Stations of the Cross — a later devotion popularized by the Franciscans.

The poetic and musical impetus of the Franciscans was not limited to the writing of formal poetry either in Latin or the vernacular. We know that besides the "high" art of the *Dies Irae* and the *Stabat Mater* there was also a flourishing popular art readily accessible to large numbers of people and readily adaptable to the religious ends of the Franciscans.

Italy had a history of popular poetry and song long before the Franciscan movement. Provençal poetry had entered Italy via Sicily in the twelfth century, spread rapidly to the North, and spawned many imitators in the noble courts by the thirteenth century. At a humbler level people sang songs, both sacred and profane, on any number of subjects. Scholars have indicated that Francis himself had some contact with this tradition of Italianized provençal, both through the tradition that was in Italy and also through the many French pilgrims who passed through Umbria on their way to Rome and the shrines of Christendom.[33]

More importantly, in Umbria, largely under the influence of the early Franciscans, appeared lay fraternities with the precise purpose of singing and acting out sacred songs on certain feastdays of the year, for the general instruction and edification of the Christian population. Records tell of these fraternities going on pilgrimage to towns and villages to perform their songs and pleas for penance. These groups of *laudesi*, as they were known, were the forerunners of the fraternities who performed the elaborate oratorios in the sixteenth century at Rome. Thus the *laudesi* can really be considered as the remote ancestors of grand opera in the Western world.[34]

It has been argued, but not with real persuasion, that the laudist tradition began with the Franciscans.[35] More recent research, however, has insisted that the tradition of fraternities of men meeting together at a local church for the purpose of singing religious praises is older than the Franciscan movement.[36] There is some evidence that such groups were active both in Florence and in Bologna before 1211. Most scholars are agreed, however, that the early Franciscans did have an immense impact on the development of this tradition and gave the movement the impetus that made it a major phenomenon in Italy, and especially in Tuscany and Umbria, in the middle years of the thirteenth century. In the year 1233, for one example, large migratory groups of *laudesi* circulated in various towns of central Italy, dressed in white (hence they were called *Bianchi*), singing and pleading for peace and reconciliation among the people. In 1260 occurred another large outpouring of this migratory sentiment, but in this instance there was the conjunction of the tradition of the *laudesi* joined with the spirit of the flagellants. This came about because of a widespread belief that the new Age of the Spirit predicted by Joachim of Flora would be ushered in after an apocalyptic ending of the "Second Age."[37] The 1260 outbreak saw groups of people going from village to town singing the popular lauds and exhorting the common people to penance both by sermon and by the personal example of the participant groups. Both the outbreak of the "Great Alleluia" in 1233 and the apocalyptic processions of 1260 were fueled to a large degree by the itinerant preaching of the early Franciscans and other mendicant friars. Their singing and extemporizing was a form of evangelizing and if the laudists became much more rigidified in times to come (confraternities of laudists in Florence persisted into the nineteenth century), their original impulse was much more charismatic and unstructured. Professor Arturo Pompeati has summed up this early laudist spirit quite well: "The laud was life then before it was poetry; it was religious life that sang, hymned, cried, admonished, and bewildered with its exalted sermons and prophecies under which bowed the heads of the penitents and fanatics with their interminable processions winding through the streets of the cities or the country lanes struck by the bright sun or dead under the winter ice, processions that went from church to church and altar to altar. The laud is the lyrical moment of this mystic life, the moment of abandon and of choral agreement."[38]

The lauds were eventually collected into books *(laudari)* and many have been found in various libraries of Italy. With rare exceptions the authors are unknown. The lauds are simple rhyming songs sung either as a monologue or, not rarely, as a dialogue. They were meant, of course, for choral singing. The study of these lauds is outside the scope of our present work (though we will treat later of Jacopone da Todi, one of the most famous of the laudists) but it would not be out of place to provide some sample verses of a typical laud. In the *Laudario di Cortone,* one of the most famous collections, there are four lauds signed by a certain Garzo (who has been tentatively identified as an ancestor of Petrarch); here are excerpts from one of them in honor of the Virgin:

> Venite a laudare
> per amore cantare
> de l'amorosa Vergine Maria

Pietosa regina sovrana
conforta la mente ch'e vana
grande medicina che sana
aiutan' per tua cortesia

cortese che fai grande doni
l'amor tou mai non ci abbandoni
pregante che tu ne perdoni
tutta la nostra villania. . . .

Come and Praise
sing with love
of the loving Virgin Mary

Holy sovereign queen
comfort the worldly soul
thou art a balm that heals
an aid through your courtesy

Kindly you grant gifts
your love will not abandon us
and we pray you to forgive
all our acts of evil. . . .[39]

Even in those few excerpts one can see some of the characteristic notes of the laud: the rhymes that are so malleable for the use of choral song; the echoes of the liturgical Office (cf. the opening lines) from which the laud had its ultimate inspiration; the direct and simple devotional character of the poetry; some of the humanizing elements in the poetry that surely must originate with the Franciscan impulse — the Franciscan notion of *cortesia* being the most characteristic in the excerpts just cited.

Besides the laudist tradition other poets in the Franciscan family used their pens for evangelical purposes and reflect other poetic traditions that had their influence on the Franciscans. The most noteworthy of these traditions was the French provençal, a tradition which had a direct impact on Saint Francis himself. One example of a Franciscan who made use of this tradition was Giacomino of Verona. He wrote two long metrical poems (which are conserved in the great library of Saint Marks at Venice) on the Heavenly Jerusalem and the Infernal Babylon. Both poems date from the late thirteenth century and are written in the quatrains of the *chansons de geste*. In these now nearly forgotten poems the "language is the language of chivalry; the saints are young and beautiful and dance before the throne of God; the dèvils are the dragons and wicked knights with whom the young princes do battle."[40]

Giacomino's two poems on the Heavenly Jerusalem and the Infernal Babylon (despite their Latin titles in the Venetian codex they are written in a dialect of Lombard Italian) are interesting in that he attempts to do poetically what was done previously in mosaics at Torcello and in the Florence baptistery: give some physical and spatial description to the world beyond our world. Paradise, for Giacomino, was a walled city with high battlements and three gates at each wall, richly decorated in pearls and gold. No sinner, even with the aid of the engines of war, could penetrate these bastions. God sits on a round throne surrounded by *santi cavalieri* (holy knights) and flanked by angels and saints who sing his praise day and night. It is, as Pompeati observed, an austere and arid view of God, but Giacomino's description of the Virgin is more humane and cordial. The madonna sits while her attendants sing the traditional hymns of Catholic praise: the *Ava Maria,* the *Salve Regina,* and the *Alma Redemptoris.* The Madonna, in turn, crowns them with garlands and hands them beautiful gifts in a spirit that makes one think of Botticelli's rendering of the Virgin:

> Dondo quella donna, tant'e gentil e granda
> ke tutti li encorona d'una nobel girlanda
> la qual e piu aolente ke n'e mosca ne ambra
> ne cijo ne altra flor ne rosa de campagna.[41]

Giacomino's description of the Infernal Babylon like Dante's description of Hell is much more vivid and descriptive. The city of Hell is full of rivers — miasmic rivers of poisonous vapors, the streets are entangled with thorns and malignant plants. Over the whole city is a metallic sky supported by a wall of stones and boulders. A never-sleeping sentinel on a tower makes sure nobody escapes from the city which is reached by a gate presided over by four demons, among them Satan and the spirit of Mohammed. The spirits who are damned there suffer, as one might expect, extremes of heat and cold, with these descriptions at times reaching the level of the burlesque. Giacomino manages to point out warning morals to his readers through his gruesome descriptions. After Giacomino tells of the soul's final passage into the infernal pit, he addresses the reader with a short, albeit fervent, homily; a homily designed to call to mind the sinner's fate and the need for him to do penance before it is too late:

> Mo v'o dar consejo, se prendro lo voli:
> fai penitentia enfina ke vui poi,
> de li vostri peccati a Deo ve repenti
> e perseverando en quello le pene fuciri.[42]

It is tempting to think that Dante knew these poems and had them in the back of his mind when he did the *Commedia*. There is no clear evidence of this fact though it is not unreasonable to think that Dante could have known the poetry during his exile in the North. At any rate, Giacomino's poetry is interesting as a comparison point with that of Dante if for no other reason than to show how superior Dante's imagination was. Giacomino was able to set forth a panoply of conventional enough delights and horrors but was unable to rise above conventional moralizing. It was left to Dante and his sense of art to move from the mere description of the otherworldly regions to a broad understanding of the soul's journey to perfection; under the paradigm of the descent and the ascent Dante put himself into the class of those other great travellers in this world and the next, Homer and Vergil, while Giacomino rested at the level of a medieval moralizer.

One poet, outside of Italy, who does deserve particular notice is the English Franciscan, John Peacham (died 1292) who not only held responsible positions in the English Franciscan Order but was also Archbishop of Canterbury from 1279 until his death in 1292. His best-known poem is a long work entitled *Philomena* written in Latin in four-lined stanzas of thirteen syllables. It was not for liturgical use but for private devotion, and is, in the opinion of Professor Raby, "personal in its emotion and filled with the new inspiration which was the secret of the Gospel of Assisi."[43]

The subject of the poem is the nightingale which, according to legend, when it learns of its death, flies to the pinnacle of a tree to pour forth song at dawn. The nightingale becomes the symbol of the soul yearning for God as it lives in this world but desires God. It sings through the hours of the day but will, like the nightingale, have its heartbreak of love, and then will return to God. Thus the pious soul, again like the nightingale, will cry out "oci! oci!" when in the contemplation of the Passion of Christ it can stand no more and seeks to leave the earth to be wrapt in the love of God:

oci, oci anima clamat in hoc statu
crebro fundens lacrimas sub hoc incolatu
laudans et glorificans magno cum conatu
Christum, qui tot pertulit suo pro reatu

(Oci, oci the soul cries in this state/
full of tears in this unhappy place/
praising and glorifying with great effort/
Christ who has accepted guilt as his own)[44]

Peacham's *Philomena* is suffused with Franciscan spirituality and
reminds one, first of all, of the *Itinerarium Mentis ad Deum* of Saint
Bonaventure in its insistence on the soul's desire to move up to God
through contemplation. It makes the object of contemplation the
Passion of Christ, and love the impetus of contemplation that moves
the soul forward. One can see a direct line that runs from the
stigmata experience of Saint Francis on Mount La Verna to
Bonaventure's *Itinerarium* (which he wrote while visiting Mount La
Verna himself) to the consummate lyrical poetry of John Peacham.

V *Jacopone Da Todi*

Of all of the laudists of the thirteenth and fourteenth centuries in
Italy the most distinctive and clearly accomplished was Jacopo
Benedetti, known more familiarly as Fra Jacopone da Todi
(1230/36? - 1306). His life is of the very stuff of romance. Jacopone
was born into an ancient and noble family of the Umbrian hill town
of Todi. About his early life we know comparatively little. We do
know that he was a trained lawyer and practiced that profession in
his home town after a university career in Bologna. In his early
manhood he married a woman named Vanna who came from a dis-
tinguished family, the Coldimozzo. According to an ancient *Vita* of
Jacopone (but one that was written long after his own lifetime and
thus much prone to hagiographical accretions), he and his wife were
at a party given by some friends when a balcony collapsed killing his
wife and some other guests. When preparing his wife's body for
burial, Jacopone discovered that under her fine dress was a penitential hairshirt that she wore close to her body. This discovery, coupled
with the shock of his wife's death, profoundly changed the course of
his life. He gave up both his patrimony and his legal career to
become a wandering mendicant and man of penance (cf. *lauda* 53:

gir bezocone)[45] in the environs of his home town. He spent ten years in this form of life, performing penance, accepting humiliations, and living as a beggar, until, in 1278, he requested and was granted admission into the Franciscan Order.

Given his temperament, and the life style that he had followed for the previous ten years, it is not surprising that Jacopone would have been immediately attracted to the Spiritual wing of the Franciscans, i.e., to that group of Franciscans who attempted to live according to the most rigorous interpretation of the life of poverty as they interpreted it from the spirit and writings of Saint Francis himself. The Spirituals were not only fiercely opposed to the mitigations of the Conventuals, but were also bitterly critical of the corruption, pretensions, and political intrigues of the Roman Church as a whole.

The election of the saintly hermit Celestine V to the papacy in 1294 gave some hope to the Spirituals that they would be allowed to constitute a separate wing of the followers of Saint Francis but Jacopone, who was curiously realistic about the chances of this otherworldly recluse from the Abruzzi to survive the intrigues of Rome, voiced his hesitancy about the capacities of the new pope in a laud addressed to the pontiff (*Que farai, Pier da Morrone?* lauda 74). Jacopone was, of course, right in being dubious. The same year that he was elected Celestine resigned, giving way to a far stronger personality, Boniface VIII. Celestine's resignation was stigmatized by Dante as the *gran rifiuto* and earned for the saintly hermit (later canonized by the Church) a place in the anteroom of Dante's Hell with the other vacillators: people neither good enough for heaven or bad enough for hell.[46]

The newly elected Boniface had little sympathy for the Spirituals and less for those who had been the partisans of the previous pontiff. In turn, the Spirituals loathed the schemingly devious pope. Jacopone went so far as to write that a new Lucifer had ascended the papal throne and that, as a result, blasphemy was spreading across the world: *Lucifero novello a sedere en papato/lengua de blasfemia ch'el mondo ai nvenenato* (lauda 83). However, the opposition of Jacopone was soon to turn from mere literary invective to a more active form of opposition.

Jacopone was one of three friars who signed the Declaration of Longhezza (May 10, 1297) which had been inspired by two brothers of the Colonna family, the cardinals, Jacopo and Pietro Colonna. The declaration declared the papal election of Boniface null and void because of its irregularities and simoniacal character. The pope's answer to this challenge was not long in coming: thirteen days after the declaration was made public Boniface issued the bull *Lapis Abscissus* excommunicating all the signers of the declaration. He then sent an army against the Colonna stronghold at Palestrina outside Rome, where the signers, Jacopone included, had taken refuge. The Colonnas held out against the papal siege for over a year and a half but, according to Dante's telling of the tale, they were betrayed by Guido da Montefeltro who advised the pope to offer terms to the besieged which would sound generous and then simply not honor the pledge (cf. *lunga promessa con l'attender corto*, Inf. XXVII, 110). Pope Boniface did exactly that. For his part in the betrayal, Guido was placed by Dante with the evil counselors and Boniface, stigmatized by Dante as the New Prince of the Pharisees (*lo principe dei novi Farisei, ibid.*, 85) would have his own place in Hell in the future.

Jacopone was taken to Rome, tried before an ecclesiastical court, and found guilty. He was expelled from the Franciscan Order, his excommunication was continued, and he was condemned to perpetual imprisonment in solitary confinement. He was to be confined in a convent of Franciscans hostile to the Spirituals and, though this is not fully established, most scholars place his confinement at the convent of San Fortunato in his native town of Todi. While in prison Jacopone twice addressed the pope in poems begging to be absolved of his excommunication (cf. *per grazia te pete/che me dichi 'absolvete'* lauda 55; the other poem to Boniface is #67), either by a personal gesture of the pope or through the agency of an ecclesiastical intermediary. Boniface, true to his intransigent and unforgiving nature, never responded to the pleas of Jacopone. Indeed, when Boniface proclaimed the first Holy Year for 1300, the Colonnas and their cohorts were specifically excluded in the papal documents from the expected pardons and indulgences. Jacopone was freed from prison in 1303 after the death of Boniface with the election of the new pope Benedict XI. After his release, he went to the town of Collazzone and found refuge there in the Poor Clares convent of San Lorenzo; he remained at this convent until his death on Christmas night in 1306.

During all of his harried religious career Jacopone wrote poetry; even though none has survived from before the date of his conversion (1286) it is quite possible that he did write poetry all of his adult life. One of the first critical problems in the study of his poetry is to decide what can be safely attributed to his pen. There are many

early manuscripts and editions of his poetry and the early printed
books give us an inkling of the incertitude about the corpus of his
writing: a Florentine edition of his poems printed in 1490 listed one
hundred and two lauds; a Brescia edition of 1495 had one hundred
and twenty; a Venetian edition of 1617, over two hundred.[47] More
recent scholarship from the last century on has narrowed down the
corpus. Thanks to the scholarly labors of Franca Ageno (1953)[48] and,
the now definitive work of Franco Mancini in the series *Scrittori
D'Italia* (1974)[49] we have a safe estimate of the Jacoponean corpus:
Mancini lists ninety-two lauds as certainly authentic and six more as
probably coming from Jacopone's pen, including the Latin hymn
Stabat Mater which is traditionally ascribed to him.

What distinguishes Jacopone's work from the vast anonymous
literature of the laudists who preceded or were contemporary with
him is the intensely personal nature of his poetry. Most of the
anonymous laudists (and the fact that they were anonymous is not
insignificant in itself) wrote in a rather detached manner. Their compositions were meant to be for popular consumption and the collec-
tive use of the singing confraternities of the *laudesi*. For the most
part they stuck to conventional patterns of speech and kept a certain
personal aesthetic distance from their work. Jacopone, on the other
hand, "wrote for himself out of a seemingly irresistible interior
urgency."[50] Many of the extant poems were frankly autobiographical or occasioned by incidents in his stormy life (as, for example, #53,
55, 67, 68). Others express his own tortured path through the
mystical *noche oscura* where he cries out his plaint: "Love, Beloved
Love, why have you left me?" (*Amor, diletto Amore, perche m'ai
lassato?* lauda 18); other poems are the working out on paper of his
own problems; one thinks immediately of the one where he
questions himself by name: "What will you do, Fra Jacopone, now
that your test has come?" (*Que farai, fra Jacovone?* lauda 53).

If personal passion with deep involvement is one of the distinctive
marks of Jacopone's poetry, it should also be noted that his poetry is
not entirely confessional. His poetry was meant to serve as a means
of his fulfilling his ministry of preaching and example. One of the
best scholars of Jacopone, Franco Mancini, does not hesitate to compare the corpus of his writings to a collection of sermons, or better
still, a moral treatise of the medieval type. The themes of the individual poems are varied but running as a leitmotif through them
all is the desire of the soul, through the annihilating force of love, to
pass over to the mystical experience of God Himself. In that sense,

the poems of Jacopone may also be fruitfully compared to the much more systematic treatise of spirituality that also comes out of the Franciscan school: Saint Bonaventure's *Journey of the Mind to God*.[51]

If this journey of the mind and soul to God is called typically Franciscan it should also be remembered that in Jacopone it had an entirely new emphasis. For Jacopone poverty was not an espousal to a fair lady as it was for Francis. Poverty was a harsh and unremitting denial of self and a rigid ascesis; it was a despising of everything earthly and a renunciation of all that was in the world in order to purify the soul for God. In Jacopone there was none of the tender effusions toward the world of nature. Jacopone combined the insights that Francis had about poverty with the older traditions that sprung from such negative mystics as the Pseudo-Areopagite. This harsher sense of self-immolation imposed on Jacopone the need for a new vocabulary; that vocabulary, as Frugoni has noted, is characterized by such words as *affocata, consumarsi, smesuranza, enfocato;* it is vocabulary that anticipates the great mystical poetry of John of the Cross by some centuries.[52]

It is generally accepted that Jacopone's poems were meant to be read out loud and that his audience was generally going to be a restricted one. Some of the early manuscripts have an *explicit* at the head of the poems which says in Latin, *"pro consolatione et profectu novitiorum studientium"* (for the consolation and development of novice students). From this hint and others, Mancini thinks that the intended audience was generally Franciscan and, more especially, the aspirants in the order. This would explain not only the elevated mystical elements in the poetry and the didactic slant of other elements but also the fierce polemics against Franciscans of the lax observance. Jacopone is also at great pains to show Francis as having a central role in the Church at that time. For Jacopone, Francis was the man sent to do battle with the Devil who again roamed the earth. In terms that owe something to the influence of the ideas of Joachim of Flora, Jacopone sees Francis as leading the struggle that must take place before the final sweeping away of the *Ecclesia Carnalis*. It is for this reason that the Franciscans can not give up their ideal of poverty or allow themselves to be linked with the false prelates of the Church (cf. *el suddito si lega col prelate/ne la sua voluntate*. lauda 17). Jacopone wanted the Franciscans to remain pure. Even though he was a man of some culture, Jacopone distrusted intellectuals. He made his own a cry that had once been uttered by one of the closest

followers of Saint Francis, Brother Leo: "Bitterly we see that Paris
(i.e., the university) has destroyed Assisi" *(Mal vedemo Parisi, che
'ave destrutt' Asisi.* lauda 91).

Closely allied to these criticisms of his own order were his com-
plaints and strictures about the condition of the Church as a whole
and, in particular, the corruption found in the Roman Curia. Except
for the brief part of a year when Celestine V was pope, Jacopone saw
nothing but hostility to the program of the Spirituals. For this reason
"Christ weeps for the Roman Church" *(Se lamenta de la Ecclesia
romana.* lauda 29). He described the hierarchy, the universities, the
clerics as all losing sight of Christ and taking a false road *(multi de la
via se se'partute.* lauda 6). The person of Boniface VIII epitomized
for Jacopone, as he did for Dante and many of the Spirituals, the
promised antichrist who would presage the end days.

In the *Laudario* of Jacopone one can trace the theme of the
mystical ascent of the soul to God through the path of self-
annihilation described in the context of the Franciscan ideal of absolute poverty. A corollary of this theme is the social criticism
directed both to the Conventual Franciscans and the Roman Curia.
Beyond that it is difficult to see any apparent interior structure to the
Laudario as a whole. Evelyn Underhill's attempt to put the lauds
into a strict chronological order has not found favor with scholars.[53]
The first thirty-three lauds (in Mancini's edition) always appeared in
the same order in most ancient manuscripts and may constitute a
"Protolaudario" that Jacopone himself may have constructed;
scholars are not insensitive to the fact that there are thirty-three
poems, number symbolism being significant for Jacopone as it was
for Dante. Yet even these thirty-three poems show no common
thread or theme. Thus, there are poems on the love of Christ
Crucified (lauda 2); on penance (lauda 10); on the five senses (lauda
19); on the petitions of the Lord's Prayer (lauda 22), etc. Furthermore, one is struck by the sheer didactic nature of some of the poems
that seem to have little to do with the others except to serve some
moral purpose tied to the general program of the ascetical life. Thus,
one of his lauds (#45) is a preachment against feminine fashion;
women who adorn themselves to be alluring to men are compared to
"*el basilisco serpente [che] eccide om cel vedere*" (the basilisk who
would kill men by looking at them).

One can ask whether the poetry of Jacopone ever reached a wider
audience in his lifetime than that of his Franciscan confreres. More
generally, one can inquire if the poems were used by the confrater-

nities of laudists who were then active all over Umbria and Tuscany. Generally speaking, the lauds are not found in the catalogs or song books of the confraternities — with one exception. Laud 61 *(Quando t'alegri)* has been discovered in a number of laudist manuscripts as being part of their repertory. The laud itself is a macabre *memento mori* in which a living person dialogues with one who is already dead. It is a poem that would be a "natural" for the laudist since it would permit antiphonal recitation between two voices in the style of a recitative *danse macabre* with one voice asking "Where are your shining eyes *(L'occhi cusi depurati)* and "Where is your well-coifed hair?" *(capo cusi pettenato)* to be answered by another that "my eyes that have so sinned have now been lost" and "the skin from my head has fallen." The poem ends, characteristically enough, with the plea that the worldly man *(omo mundanus)* should contemplate this pitiable scene because before long it will be the fate of every man alive *(Pensate, folle, che a mmano a mmano/tu sirai messo en gran estratura).*

There is also some internal evidence that Jacopone expected his lauds to have a wider audience and so constructed them with that purpose in mind. Jacopone's meter, by and large, is quite similar to that of the other laudists, who are, in turn, indebted to the popular secular balladers of the day. Their ballads, have an opening refrain that is followed by a series of strophes with the last verse of the strophe repeating the meter of the refrain with which the laud began. Beyond that, the opening lines of some of the lauds indicate that they were to be heard by a large audience rather than an individual or select few. Thus three lauds (# 7, 10, 57) begin with the words *Audite una'ntenzona* (listen to a debate). The lauds then follow the convention of the *'ntenzone* with a dialogue between the soul and the body or honor and shame or two persons of differing moral standards. Yet another laud (# 86) in its opening lines, actually encourages the audience, to sing praises *(a lauda fare):*

> A l'amor ch'e vinuto
> en carne nnuise dare
> andiamo laude fare
> e canto con onore

> (To that love which became flesh as a gift to us/
> Let us praise and sing with honor)

One final suggestion that scholars have made, though tentatively, concerns the wider influence of Jacopone's poetry. At least two art historians have advanced the thesis that there is some connection between the poetry of Jacopone and the frescos that Cimabue did for the Basilica of San Francis at Assisi.[54] Cimabue (1204? - 1302) was a younger contemporary of Jacopone and his work may be seen both in the upper and lower churches of the great Franciscan basilica. Cimabue shows an evident indebtedness to the Italo-Byzantine tradition which then held sway in Italy but, as scholars point out, he made the first consistent efforts to go beyond that tradition in new directions. That new path is best illustrated in the fresco of the Crucifixion that he did in the upper church of the Basilica of Saint Francis. Cimabue illustrates this scene in a dramatic swirl of emotion with angels fluttering at the side of the Cross in an agitated frenzy. The figure of the Virgin and Saint John the Evangelist are dramatically isolated from the crowd who point up at the dying Christ. It is unique and moves beyond the conventions of Italo-Byzantine crucifixions. Mario Salmi has pointed out that just at the time Cimabue was working at Assisi there were fresh memories there, and in all of Umbria, of the penitential groups of *laudesi* who walked the whole faction-torn region calling for peace, reconciliation, and fraternal love in the name of the Crucified Jesus.

There is no direct evidence of a connection between Jacopone's poetry and the frescos of Cimabue. Jacopone himself, given his fierce love of poverty and his hatred for ostentation, would probably not have approved of the artistic decoration of the church where Francis was buried. But, at least for some scholars, the violent poetry of Jacopone would have been a natural and plausible source of inspiration for a figure as passionate and involved as Cimabue who was "without a doubt profoundly impressed by the waves of penitent singers praising 'poverty' and affirming that 'with Christ one reigns.' This climate undoubtedly nourished his masterpiece at Assisi."[55] Out of the anonymous band of laudists Jacopone emerged with a distinct style and a personal interpretation of the Christian life. In that he had a career similar to Cimabue himself.

But Jacopone da Todi is not only remembered for his possible influence on early Italian art. He is the best representative of what we might call the "proletarian wing" of the Franciscan movement. We must remember that his career was begun roughly at the time that Saint Bonaventure was changing the face of the Franciscan movement. The world of Bonaventure was not the world of Jacopone. It should be noted that he never wrote (if we make exception for the *Stabat Mater)* in the official clerical tongue of Latin. He showed little evidence of interest or even sympathy for the scholastic formulations of theological truth. He used earthy and basic terms to describe his vision of life. His poetry was often quite didactic and also oriented to the listener, both for his instruction and for his edification. This "proletarian" form of Jacopone's poetry was summarized nicely by Francesco De Sanctis:

> Jacopone's work reflects Italian life under one of its aspects more truly than those of any troubadour. He gives us the religious feeling in its first native expression; religion as it is found in the uncultivated classes, not clouded by theology or scholasticism and carried to the heights of mysticism and ecstasy. He communes directly with God, the Virgin, the saints and the angels, speaks to them with domestic familiarity, and paints them with perfect freedom of imagination, with those touchingly pious and affectionate details that could only be imagined by a fancy moved by love. His chief idol is Mary, and he speaks to her with the insistence and intimacy of a person who is sure of his faith and knows that he loves.[56]

De Sanctis wrote from the perspective of Hegelian idealism and romanticism and it was natural enough for him to emphasize the earthiness of Jacopone's poetry. But this side of Jacopone must always be read in tension with the tradition of his poetry that underlies the tradition of apophatic or negative mysticism that we have already mentioned: the poetry of annihilation and the prayer of the dark night of the soul. Therefore it is incorrect to think of Jacopone — as did so many critics of the last century — as the "fool of Christ" or the "troubadour of Our Lady" if we mean that in any whimsical or light sense. This becomes quite clear when we examine the dynamic underlying one of Jacopone's most famous lauds, (#70) *Donna de Paradiso.* The theme of the poem is the same as that of the hymn *Stabat Mater:* the lament of the Virgin as she sees the Passion of her Son. In the middle of the poem there is a dialogue between Jesus and his Mother (referred to familiarly as "Mamma" in the poem). What makes the poem so personal and so dynamic is the fusion of two typically Jacoponean motifs: the profundity of sorrow and the immensity of love. Jesus from the Cross insists that his mother stay behind while she insists that she wants to die with Him *(voglio teco morire).* Mary accepts the will of Christ and the poem ends with a long keening lament that summarizes both her sense of maternal loss and the sorrow of the sight of the Cross:

Figlio bianco e biondo	My fair and blond son
figlio iocondo.	My son so light hearted
figlio perche t'a el mundo	My son, why has the world,
figlio cusi sprezzatio?	My son, so despised you?

In this laud and many others like it we can see that inner Jacoponean dynamic at work: he is able to write from the level of our common experience but in the transfer of that experience to the spiritual level he underscores the basic metaphysics of love, suffering, aspiration, and the limits of the human experience. This overriding love (analyzed at length in laud # 25) is the source of all of Jacopone's mysticism. Love (in laud # 25) puts the body in a state of submission and quiet and leads the soul to God. This doctrine of love, often suspect for its quietistic and pantheistic impulses by earlier Catholic critics (e.g., Frederic Ozanam), is understood now to reach back from the Victorines mystics of France through John Scotus Erigena who was the translator and disseminator of the writings of the mystical theology of the Pseudo-Dionysius.

Jacopone, then, stands at the confluence of two traditions: the reverent humanism of Francis of Assisi which attempts to see the truths of Christianity not as abstract statements but as existent realities and the earlier mysticism of the Pseudo-Dionysius that understands a "beyond" in the life of prayer. Jacopone has the ability to concretize his religious experience but has a sense of the secrecy and the ineffable profundity of the life of prayer where the images of our history are swallowed up in the ecstatic union of man with God. Jacopone is *sui generis;* he is neither the attractive Poor Man of Assisi nor is he the easy synthesizer of scholasticism and Franciscan mysticism as was Saint Bonaventure. He somehow managed to combine in his poetry both the Franciscan *dolcezza* and the asperity of the *via negativa.*

CHAPTER 3

The Legendae of Saint Francis

THIS chapter will attempt to give a broad panoramic view of the most important works that were written after the death of Saint Francis of Assisi on his life and significance. This chapter is necessary for two reasons. The first, and most obvious reason, is that the various lives of the saint contain much information that has come down to us from persons who were either intimate friends of the saint or from those — like Thomas of Celano and Saint Bonaventure — who actively searched out persons who could provide firsthand information. As we have already noted, Francis, with rare exceptions such as the *Testament,* was quite reticent about himself. His writings were either of a devotional nature or concerned with the problems of the Franciscan brotherhood. Hence it is in the writings that emerged after his death that one must search for clues about his day-by-day life and thought. There is, of course, a risk in this as the following pages will make clear. Francis was a controversial figure and the books about him were burdened at times with either polemical or edificatory slants. It has been the task of the historian to disengage the real Francis from the pious interpolations of the various writers. This is a task that historians have been engaged in for a long time and if the work is not yet completely finished, nonetheless, some progress has been made. This book is not primarily concerned with the many thorny problems of Franciscan historiography but it is impossible totally to avoid such questions as the historical reliability of some of the works under discussion or the interrelationship of some of the works. The so-called Franciscan Question is extremely complex and it will be possible to discuss it only in a passing fashion so as to give the reader a sense of the intricacies involved.

The second reason why we must give some attention to the books written about Saint Francis after his death is because of their great impact on the development of what is called the "proto-Renaissance." It has been recognized since the last century, largely due to the efforts of such scholars as Ozanam, Thode, and Sabatier, that the Franciscan mystique created a profound force for change in the thirteenth and fourteenth centuries, not only in the field of popular religion but also in the area of the visual arts (especially in painting and, to a lesser extent, in architecture) and *belles lettres*. We hope to give some indication of these changes in this chapter.

Finally, one must recognize the vast literature generated during the hundred or so years after the death of the saint and one must make a rational selection from among this output. This chapter will use as its starting point the *Sacrum Commercium* which most scholars think was written within two years after the death of the saint and will consider the *Fioretti* as the final point of the period. We have not mentioned in this survey the amount of philosophical material written by Franciscans, or the large number of liturgical writings generated as the cult of Saint Francis grew both within and outside the order. Where this material has some relevance for our discussion it is noted and appropriate bibliographical notations are given for those who wish to pursue these matters further. We have, as part V of this chapter, included a section on the more famous of the early Franciscan chronicles, not because they deal directly with Saint Francis but because they give the reader some sense of the development of the Franciscan *religio*. One understands the need to do this once a study of early Franciscan history is started. The polemics that undergird the documents studied in this chapter deal, at least partially, with the fundamental question of how the brotherhood should ideally develop to be in conformity with the spirit of Saint Francis. These chronicles give us some sense of how it actually developed.

I *The* Sacrum Commercium

There are thirteen extant codices of this beautiful allegory of the romance (which is about as close as one can come in English to the Latin word *commercium*) of Lady Poverty and Saint Francis. Six of the codices end with the note indicating that the work was completed in July, 1227. If this date is correct (and a few scholars have doubted it based largely on internal evidence), then the *Sacrum Commercium* is the very first piece of Franciscan literature written after the death of the saint.[1] The authorship of the work is a matter of some scholarly dispute. John of Parma (minister general of the Franciscans from 1247 to 1257) is named as the author in several old manuscript sources while other scholars have thought that the name should be read as John Parenti, who was minister in 1227. Other later codices have attributed the authorship to various persons ranging from Saint Anthony of Padua to Crescentius of Jesi, who was the minister general from 1244 to 1247. The Quaracchi editors and, following their tentative suggestion, Placid Hermann, have suggested Thomas of Celano on the basis of some internal evidence, especially through an analysis of the *Commercium* and Celano's *Vita Prima* (to be discussed later in this chapter).[2] There is further plausibility in this attribution since we know that Thomas was a literary figure of some note and was commissioned by Pope Gregory IX in 1228 to write the first official life of the saint. It is tempting to think that Thomas received the commission precisely because he had already demonstrated his abilities in the writing of the *Sacrum Commercium* in the previous year.

The *Sacrum Commercium* is a short allegorical prose work consisting of a brief prologue and six chapters. The prologue insists that poverty is the "foundation of all the other virtues" which stands both "in place and in name among the other evangelical virtues." Poverty has this preeminence because Christ himself was poor both in life and death; because he praised poverty before any other virtue (i.e., in the Beatitudes; cf. Matthew 5:3: Blessed are the poor in spirit, etc.); and, finally, because he counselled those who wished to follow a perfect life to live in poverty. The prologue ends noting that Francis lived in poverty all his life because he understood that poverty was the key that opened the gates of heaven.

Chapter one of the *Sacrum Commercium* opens with Francis wandering the streets of a city seeking the one "whom his heart loved." His searchings and wanderings brought no success. He finally found two old men sitting in a field at the outskirts of a city who tell him that Lady Poverty has fled to the pinnacle of a high mountain and Francis is encouraged to despoil himself of every possession in order to go and find out where she dwells. The two old men probably represent the Old and New Testaments since one quotes from the prophet Isaiah and the other from the letters of Saint Paul. Francis, along with "certain chosen companions," gives away everything and, thus denuded, goes to seek his lady.

The second chapter of the allegory depicts Francis and his companions ascending the mountain while they are being encouraged and then welcomed by Lady Poverty herself who sits at the top "reclining in her total nothingness." Francis praises Lady Poverty for her role in the unfolding of Sacred History, a role which culminated when "the Son of the most high Father became enamoured of your beauty." In the following chapter Lady Poverty praises the words of Francis and then, in turn, recounts her own story from the days of Adam to the days of the coming of Christ when He (Christ) exalted her both through his teachings and in the example of his life. Lady Poverty also praises her faithful assistant and powerful aide, Lady Persecution, though, as Lady Poverty notes, in these present days she has been banished and the people have grown complacent. Lady Poverty ends this speech by saying that although she and Lady Persecution have been nearly forgotten there has always been a faithful remnant that has cultivated the virtue of poverty.

The fourth chapter is a continuation of the speech that she had been making in chapter three but now it takes on the negative side: those who have opposed her work throughout the ages. In the first place there is Avarice but, she notes ironically, her devotees now call Avarice by a "holier name lest they should have appeared to have completely abandoned me"; the "new" name for Avarice is Discretion or Providence. Avarice, under the name of Discretion, makes pacts with the wealthy and the powerful for the sake of commodiousness or efficiency. When Avarice was unable to do her work alone she called on a faithful companion, Sloth, who "is loath to begin good works and to complete that which she has begun." Lady Poverty then ends this speech by recalling the successes that Avarice and Sloth have had among mankind.

Chapters five and six provide the *denouement* of the allegory. Lady Poverty invites Francis to follow her and he responds with alacrity to her invitation: "She [Poverty] could then restrain herself no longer and she ran and embraced them all, giving to each the kiss of peace . . . " Francis then led Lady Poverty down from the mountain at "about the sixth hour" (the reference is to the hour of the crucifixion of Christ on Mount Calvary, cf. John 19:14) to the plain below where they dwelt. In the final chapter Francis and his companions offer Lady Poverty a banquet of water and bread served under the poorest of circumstances. The banquet ends with Lady Poverty counselling the brothers always to persevere in the ideals of poverty.

The *Sacrum Commercium* is a lovely medieval allegory that took its inspiration from Francis's own personification of poverty as a lady with whom he had had a romance and had wed, a story later recounted by Thomas of Celano in the *Vita Prima* and the unknown author of the *Legend of the Three Companions.* The poverty of which this allegory speaks is not merely the absence of material goods but includes the whole theological substructure of self-effacement and the total giving of self — themes that are part of the common font of Christian ascetical literature with roots back in the Pauline literature. For the author of the *Sacrum Commercium,* the ultimate exemplar of this poverty was Christ himself who accepted the poverty of the human condition and, in a final act of giving, also gave up his life on the cross.

While it would be an exaggeration to say — as did Paul Sabatier, for example — that Dante relied exclusively on this short allegory for the writing of canto xi of the *Paradiso,* most Danteans are convinced that Dante did know the work and made use of it in writing his tribute to Saint Francis. It is quite possible that Dante knew the contents of the *Sacrum Commercium* through a book written by the Spiritual Franciscan, Ubertino da Casale. Ubertino had incurred the displeasure of his Franciscan superiors because of his espousal of extreme views regarding poverty and had been forced to retire to La Verna sometime after 1300. There he wrote a book called the *Arbor Vitae Crucifixae* drawing copiously on the *Sacrum Commercium.*[3] Dante knew of Ubertino and his career since there is an oblique reference to him in *Paradiso* xii, 124.

In canto xi of the *Paradiso* Saint Thomas Aquinas eulogizes Francis just as, in the following canto, the Franciscan Saint Bonaventure will eulogize Saint Dominic. Drawing on the *Legenda Major* of Bonaventure (discussed later in this chapter), Dante describes Francis as entering into holy marriage with Lady Poverty at the time when Francis stripped himself naked and gave up all his possessions in the famous encounter that he had with his father before the bishop of Assisi. This Lady, Dante continues, had been deprived of her first husband (Christ) for over a thousand years (*Questa, privata del primo marito/Mille cent'anni e piu dispetta e scura* — xi, 64 - 5). Lady Poverty always remained with Francis and in time the two of them were able to attract other companions to them; Dante then names some of the earliest companions of the saint (xi, 79 - 84): Bernard of Quintavalle, Egidio, and Silvestro. Then, after recounting some of the salient events in the saint's life, Dante recalls how Francis left his companions in the care of Lady Poverty while he himself died in her lap (*del suo grembo,* xi, 115). Lady Poverty's lap is, of course, the earth itself. Francis, before his death, asked to be stripped of his clothes and placed on the naked earth for he wished to have no other coffin for his body *(e al suo corpo non valse altra bara* — xl, 117).

Dante's description of the relationship of Francis and Lady Poverty follows closely both the spirit and some of the ideas of the *Sacrum Commercium*. It is quite possible that Dante refashions in a poetic way lines taken from the prose allegory itself. Thus, in describing Lady Poverty's relationship to Christ, her first husband, Dante writes these exquisite lines:

> Dove Maria rimase giuso
> Ella [Poverty] con Cristo salse en sulla croce
> (While Mary remained below
> she mounted the cross with Christ, *par.* xi, 71 - 2)

That image is reminiscent of the following lines found in the *Sacrum Commercium:*

You did not leave him unto death, even the death on the cross. And on the cross itself, when he hung there naked, his arms outstretched, his hands and feet pierced, you suffered with him, so that nothing in him should appear more glorious than you.[4]

Besides its literary influence on Dante, the *Sacrum Commercium* is the probable source of the famous fresco of the wedding of Saint Francis and Lady Poverty over the main altar of the lower church of the Basilica of Saint Francis at Assisi. Long attributed to Giotto, but now simply called "Giottoesque" it is one of the four frescos over the main altar (the so-called "quattro vele") that are meant to exalt the evangelical virtues and to show Francis in heavenly glory. The fresco of the mystic marriage of Francis and poverty depicts a resplendent Christ joining the saint and Lady Poverty in a mystic nuptial bond symbolized by Christ joining the stigmatized hand of Francis to that of the allegorical female figure of Poverty. She stands to the left of Christ with her bare feet encircled with brambles and thorns, dressed in a patched and tattered gown. Francis is depicted to the right and just in front of Christ who is receiving her hand.

The theme of a "mystic marriage" is a fairly ancient one in Christianity and ultimately derives from the allegorical exegesis of the *Song of Songs* from the Old Testament. In painting, the theme usually depicts the marriage of Christ and some saint, more often than not, a female saint, i.e., the mystic marriage of Christ and Saint Catherine of Siena or, more rarely, Christ and the Church or, rarer still, Christ and the Virgin Mary.[5] The mystic marriage of a saint and an allegorical figure at this date (the fresco dates from shortly after 1300?) is fairly unique even though it had its artistic influence on later depictions of a wide variety of subjects. This particular fresco, then, must be traced back to the cavalier imagery employed by Francis himself and, more likely, to the *Sacrum Commercium* and its repetition in the *Arbor Vitate Crucifixae* where it gets a full literary treatment.

II *The* Legendae *of Thomas of Celano*

Francis Bernadone was canonized a saint at Assisi by Pope Gregory IX on July 16, 1228. On that day, or a few days before, the pope commissioned Brother Thomas of Celano to write a life of the saint. Thomas of Celano was not a member of the original Franciscan fraternity. It is thought that he entered the order around 1215 and we know that he spent most of his Franciscan career in Germany, though it is possible that he spent time in Assisi during the last two years of the saint's life. There has been some speculation as to why Thomas was chosen to be the official biographer of the saint. It may have been because he had already demonstrated literary abilities (if he was, in fact, the author of the *Sacrum Commercium*, as some have suggested); or because of his education which does show through in his writing; or because both the pope and the ministers of the order wanted someone who was relatively distant from the nascent factionalism and discontent that had begun to plague the Franciscans even before the death of the saint.

Thomas completed his work in short order.[6] According to a note appended to a fourteenth century manuscript of the *Vita Prima* Thomas presented his work to Pope Gregory on February 25, 1229. Even if that date is open to question, the work must have been completed before May 25, 1230, because Thomas makes no mention of the solemn translation of the body of Francis from the Assisi church of San Giorgio where it had been originally buried to the new basilica in Assisi which had been built to receive the body.

What were the sources that Thomas used for the writing of his biography? He undoubtedly compiled material from the anecdotes and reminiscences of the citizens of Assisi who were contemporaries of Francis and those members of the Franciscans who were closest to the saint during his life. He probably consulted Brother Elias of Cortona who had been the vicar of the order since 1221 and who was, at the time of his writing, the head of the order. The pope himself (the

former Cardinal Hugolin) could have supplied details since he had
been an early friend and adviser to the young order as well as an intimate friend of Saint Clare.[7] Thomas probably also consulted the official *Acta* of the canonization though we do not know what influence they had since the *Acta* have been lost. Finally, as we have
seen in an earlier chapter, Thomas quotes from the writings of the
saint which means that he also had access to some of these writings,
if not all of them.

One must not think of the *Vita* that Thomas wrote in terms of a
modern biography. The *Vita* belongs to the medieval genre of the
legenda, i.e., the account of the deeds of a saint meant for the
edification of a public who would hear the account read *(legenda:*
from Latin *legere* — to read) at public gatherings or selections read
at liturgical services. It would be anachronistic to expect Thomas to
handle the sources with the care or the judgment of a modern scien-
tific biographer. Thomas was a hagiographer and was subject both to
the credulity of his age and the pressures of those who had commissioned him to write, i.e., the pope and his own religious
superiors. Thus, as John Moorman has noted,[8] he passes over any account of either the dissensions within the order, or the abandonment
of the early ideals of poverty, or the struggles concerning the writing
of the *Rule of 1221* and the *Rule of 1223.* Nor are there many direct
references to the oldest companions of the saint who were not at one
mind with the ambitious plans of Elias of Cortona, then the head of
the Franciscans.

The book that emerges from the pen of Thomas is "conventional,
stereotyped, and authoritative."[9] The *Vita* reveals that Thomas is
completely at home with Sacred Scripture, which he weaves into his
narrative almost to the point of tedium, and had more than a passing
knowledge of the ancient writers, both classical and Christian.
Thomas was also well versed in the rhetorical conventions of his age.
As Placid Hermann notes, he readily uses similes, metaphors, contrast, and antithesis, and constructs his sentences in line with the
rhythmical patterns of the medieval *cursus.*[10]

The prologue to the *Vita Prima* sets out the plan of the book.
Thomas tells us that he had arranged his work into three separate
"books." The first of these books will follow the chronological order
of the saint's life and will intersperse that account with some of the
miracles that were performed during the lifetime of the saint. The
second book recounts the events from 1224 to 1226 — years in which
the *Canticle of Brother Sun* was composed, Christmas at Greccio was

celebrated, and the stigmata was received on Mount La Verna. The third book describes the miracles performed through the intercession of Francis after his death and ends with a description of his canonization in 1228. A short, one-paragraph, epilogue states that not everything about the life of the saint had been written down but that which had been recounted "had been written for the glory of God."

The first book of the *Vita Prima*, subdivided into thirty chapters, treats of the events of the life of Francis from his early youth (a time in which "he squandered and wasted his time miserably") to the year of his conversion (which Thomas places in 1207) through the years of the growth of the order from the earliest days of his first companions up until the 1223 celebration of Christmas at Greccio where Francis constructed a crèche (reputed to be the first one) for the Christmas Eve midnight Mass. Many of the events immortalized in the later art of the Duecento and Trecento are first set down in writing in this first part of the book: the encounter with his father before the bishop of Assisi; his rebuilding of the church of San Damiano; the early companions who went with him to Rome to get confirmation of their rule from Pope Innocent III; the missionary journey; the visit to the Sultan at Damietta during the crusade there. There is no doubt that the portrait that Thomas wished to draw — and he drew it very well given the canons of his time — was that of an impeccable man of God who not only sought his own perfection but served as an exemplar and animator of those who chose to follow him. One point that should be emphasized about the events recorded by Celano is the author's continued insistence on the way in which the life of Francis paralleled that of Christ. He did this by the use of scriptural texts in his narrative in such a way as to remind the reader that the Gospel passages once applied to Christ and are now, *mutatis mutandis*, applied to Francis. Thus, to cite one example, when Francis finished his sermon to the birds, someone in the crowd cried out "Truly this man is a saint and a friend of the Most High," echoing a somewhat similar cry made at the time of the crucifixion of Christ. The point of establishing such conformities and parallels with the life of Christ would get greatly exaggerated in the Spirituals' attempt to show that Francis was the "New Man" predicted for the coming of the final days and would also get greatly exaggerated in the adulation that Franciscans showed their founder. A fourteenth-century book called the *De Conformitate Vitae B. Francisci ad Vitam D. N. Jesu* by Fra Bartholomew of Pisa[11] carried this tendency to an extreme and it was that book which brought so much odium down on the heads of the friars in and after the Reformation period.

One particular element in the book that deserves mention is the portrait that Thomas provides of the saint himself. It is remarkably close to a very old fresco portrait preserved in the Benedictine monastery of Subiaco and thought to have been done either from life at the time of the saint's visit there or by someone who actually knew him. Celano's description deserves quotation:

He was of medium height, close to shortness; his head was moderate in size and round, his face a bit long and prominent, his forehead smooth and low, his eyes were of moderate size, black and sound, his hair was black, his eyebrows straight, his nose symetrical, thin and straight; his ears were upright but small, his temples smooth. His speech was peaceable, fiery and sharp; his voice was strong, sweet, clear and sonorous. His teeth were set close together, even, and white; his lips were small and thin, his beard black but not bushy. His neck was slender, his shoulders straight, his arms short, his hands slender, his fingers long, his legs were thin, his feet small. His skin was delicate, his flesh very sparse. He wore rough garments, he slept but briefly, he gave most generously.[12]

Book two of the *Vita Prima* treats the last two years of the saint's life in some detail even though Celano notes that in this account (which consists of ten chapters) he "intends to note down only those things which were of greater importance so that they who wish to say more about them may always be able to find something they can add." The great events of this period which Celano treats are the stigmata at Mount La Verna, the last illness of Francis, and his death. These events are described in the briefest manner without much narrative detail but with a fair amount of homiletic and devotional material. The event of the stigmata, for example, is recounted in a skeletal way (i.e., two years before his death while Francis was meditating on Mount La Verna a seraph appeared to him and imprinted on his body the wounds of Christ) unlike later versions (such as the *Five Considerations of the Stigmata* appended to the *Fioretti*) which provide many particulars.

What is more interesting about this part of the *Vita* are the omissions. Celano does allude to the *Canticle of Brother Sun* in passing but gives no particulars to its composition in the last year of the saint's life. Nor does he make any reference to the *Testament* of Francis. This latter omission was probably inspired by political considerations. The *Testament*, as we have seen in the first chapter, was a strong affirmation about poverty and a command that the friars accept no papal privilege. Since the pope commissioned Celano to write and since Elias of Cortona was minister of the order (with a far different idea of what constituted poverty), it would have been exceedingly impolitic of Celano to have brought up that most embarrassing of documents.

Book three of the *Vita Prima* is the shortest of all, containing just two long chapters. The first chapter recounts the events of the canonization of the saint: the sermon of Pope Gregory, the reading out of the life and miracles of the saint, the proclamation of sanctity, and, finally, the solemn *Te Deum*. The second chapter consists of a long series of miracle stories performed through the intercession of the saint after his death: healings from sickness, the cleansing of lepers, the exorcism of possessed persons, etc. One example of these stories will suffice to give an idea of their general flavor:

A certain girl from Gubbio had hands so crippled that she had lost the use of all her members for a year. Her nurse carried her with a waxen image to the tomb of the most blessed Father Francis to obtain the grace of health. After she had been there eight days, one day all her limbs were restored to their original use, so that she was fit again for her former tasks.[13]

This then was the official life of the saint that was circulated about the Christian world until Celano was to do a second version (the *Vita Secunda*) in 1246. During the intervening years, Celano's *Vita Prima* was the source for a number of other works on the saint's life, but they were more or less a rehash of what Celano had written. At the request of a certain Brother Benedict (usually identified as Brother Benedict of Arezzo who had served as Minister General in Greece until 1237) Thomas of Celano wrote a much shorter version of the *Vita Prima* for liturgical use. The work, *Legenda Ad Usum Chori (Legend for Choir Use)*,[14] is a word-for-word adaptation of the *Vita Prima*, adding only a short description of the transferral of the body of the saint to the new basilica, an incident omitted in the *Vita Prima*. Around the year 1235 Julian of Speyer compiled a *Vita Sancti Francisci*[15] which is almost totally dependent on Celano's *Vita*. In the same period Henry of Avanches did a version of the *Vita Prima* called the *Legenda Versificata*[16], and there has been preserved a verse résumé of a *Vita* written by a papal notary, John of Celano (no relation to Thomas), called *Quasi Stella Matutina*, but John of Celano's *Vita* itself has been lost.[17]

At the general chapter of the Franciscans held at Genoa in 1244 the general of the order, Crescentius of Jesi, requested that every friar in the world who knew anything with certainty about the life and deeds of Francis send such information to him. Among those responding to this request were three friars (Leo, Ruffino, and Angelo) who had been among the oldest and most intimate friends and companions of the saint (Leo had been Francis's confessor). The three had gathered at the hermitage of Greccio where they made a collection of reminiscences and stories about Francis which they sent with a covering letter dated August 11, 1246, to the general with the hope that some of this material would be included in any new *Legenda* written about the saint. This material was handed over to Thomas of Celano with the order to write a new life of the saint based on his own researches, the memorial of the three brothers from Greccio, and, presumably, other material that had been sent in as requested by Crescentius in 1244. As usual, Thomas worked with some haste and his *Vita Secunda*[18] was ready for approval for the general chapter which was held at Lyons, France, in 1247. The confirmation was made by Brother John of Parma who had replaced the deposed Crescentius of Jesi.

The prologue of the *Vita Secunda* is especially pertinent for an understanding of this book because Thomas clearly allies himself with the brothers who had sent in new material for a life of the saint. Thomas writes that "we set down in writing," the words and deeds of the saint because ". . . they were better known to us than to the rest because of our close association with him and our mutual intimacy." Thomas of Celano was not an intimate friend of the saint so it is evident that he has here reflected the intentions of Leo, Ruffino, and Angelo. The prologue then goes on to say that the book will relate some facts about the saint's conversion that had not been noted in the earlier work but will be most concerned to show what the will of Francis was for himself and his companions. Finally, the prologue notes, "miracles are inserted, as occasion for inserting them presents itself." The whole book, the prologue concludes, is dedicated to Crescentius of Jesi.

The most fruitful way to approach the *Vita Secunda* is to compare and contrast it with the previous *Vita* of Thomas. What emerges from such a comparison is the feeling that Thomas no longer felt bound by the restraint of prudence that was imposed on him in writing the first life of Francis. The Franciscan Order was being convulsed by interior strife and it is clear that Thomas's sympathies were

with those who held up the older, more rigorous, views of poverty
and simplicity in the Franciscan way of life. Questions that were
either skirted or ignored altogether in the *Vita Prima* are now openly
discussed and it is clear that Thomas wished to express, as openly as
he could, just what the mind of Francis was on these matters. Thus,
in the *Vita Secunda*, he included a series of short anecdotes on
poverty in which Francis is described as ordering his brethren to tear
down a house made of stone erected at the Portiuncula for a chapter
meeting; how he forbade the building of stone dwellings; how he
similarly drove out brothers (including a sick one) from a finely constructed convent at Bologna. All of these tales carried an implicit
judgment both against the elaborate basilica built at Assisi and the
unending program of erecting friaries and convents then going on in
the order. Another issue about which the conservative wing had
strong opinions was the question of higher education. Francis had
little education himself, and while he showed respect for the work of
theologians and preachers, his own attitude was profoundly anti-
intellectual. The conservative wing of the Franciscans held this same
attitude and was hostile to the university. We have already seen that
Jacopone da Todi echoes the sentiments of the early friars that Paris
(i.e., the university) was destroying Assisi. In the *Vita Secunda* this
anti-intellectual attitude is strongly reinforced through stories.
Celano records how Francis warned his friars against undue curiosity
about books (cap. xxxii); how he meditated on Scriptures that he had
memorized instead of "wandering about through a thousand
treatises" (cap. lxviii); how Francis explained a passage from the
prophets to a Dominican friar in such a way that the learned man
found his own learning to "crawl on its own belly on the ground"
(cap. lxix); how Francis rebuked a young friar who had encouraged
the saint to read more (cap. lxxi).

The *Second Life* is less biographical than the *First Life*. The first
part of the work (Book One) consists of seventeen chapters that deal
mainly with the early life of the saint. Passages in this part, omitted
in the early work of Celano, have become justly famous as a part of
both Franciscan legend and iconography: Francis and the speaking
crucifix at San Damiano; the selling of his father's cloth at Foligno
for alms for the poor; the dramatic encounter of Francis and his
father before the bishop of Assisi — a scene immortalized by Giotto
in the Bardi chapel of the church of Santa Croce in Florence. Book
Two of the *Vita Secunda* has a short opening prologue that explains
that the book will contain some "memories whereby the saint may

be commended and our slumbering affections stirred anew." In one hundred and sixty chapters anecdotes are told about the saint, often employing the rubric "we remember," an indication that Celano was making use of the source material that had been sent in at the request of the general chapter. With the exception of the last four chapters (where the author picks up a narrative line again and tells of the last days of the saint and of the canonization and translation of his body to the basilica prepared for it) the chapters are arranged rather roughly according to topics. Thus, for example, chapters li-lx deal, in a series of stories, with his compassion for the poor; chapters lxviii-lxxix treat of his intuitive knowledge of the Scriptures. Perhaps the most charming of these groupings (and certainly the most influential in terms of his public *persona* through the ages and his influence on the visual arts) are those anecdotes that deal with the relationship of Francis and the world of nature. "In all beautiful things," Celano writes, "He saw Beauty itself." The account goes on to say that he loved candles, flames, and all forms of light because it reminded him of the love of God. He gave instructions that sugar and wine be set out for the bees in wintertime. "He called all animals by the name of 'brother' though among the animals, he preferred the most gentle." Charming stories tell of a pheasant that Francis tamed, of a falcon that would call him for the hours of prayer, and of Francis exhorting a tree cricket to sing for the glory of God.

The portrait of Saint Francis that emerges from the *Vita Secunda* is less stereotyped and formal than that of the *Vita Prima*. Celano does not overly emphasize the miraculous in the second biography and he does not hesitate to describe the anguish and the disappointment that Francis felt in his last years as he saw his simple ideals compromised or betrayed. In his last illness Francis cries out, "Who are those who have snatched my order and that of my brothers out of my hands?" (cap. cxli); he curses those who wear soft garments without necessity (cap. xxxix); he predicts the censure and disrespect of the world when the brethren depart from the ideals of poverty (cap. xl); he chides a novice who distributed his goods to relatives rather than to the poor, calling him "brother fly" (cap. xlix); in an entire section Francis speaks out against unworthy brethren (cap. cxvi *et seq*).

As we have already noted above, Celano only dealt with the miracles of Francis in the *Vita Secunda* in a perfunctory manner. This was seen as a defect in the book, especially since the *Vita Prima* itself contained a whole section on miracles. Because of this lacuna, John of Parma, then the Minister General of the Franciscans, ordered Thomas to compile a list of miracles in the form of a treatise. Celano complied with this request and in the years 1250 - 53 completed the *Tractatus de Miraculis Beati Francisci (Treatise on the Miracles of Blessed Francis).*[19] The *Tractatus* is not all that original a work. About one third of it is a repetition of stories already recounted in the *Vita Prima* with the addition of some other unpublished stories that Celano had collected. A few biographical observations also appear in the *Tractatus,* most of which were already recounted in the two *Lives.* There are, however, some new stories mentioning Lady Jacopa of Settesoli, a noble Roman friend of Francis, who had given the saint hospitality in Rome and whom Francis summoned to his deathbed.

Although most critics are in agreement that Thomas of Celano did write the *Vita Secunda,* despite the repeated use of plurals that indicate massive borrowings from the memorial sent in by the three friars from Greccio, the question of what happened to that material itself has never been totally answered. It is indeed the most disputed question in Franciscan studies and has been the subject of historical and philological investigation for nearly one hundred years. There is a book called the *Legenda Trium Sociorum (The Legend of the Three Companions)* which has very early manuscript support and which is usually found with the original letter of the three brothers attached at the head of it.[20] For a long time it was thought that this was the original memorial sent by Leo, Ruffino, and Angelo. It is now generally felt that the letter was superimposed on the manuscript and that the *Legenda Trium Sociorum,* while containing some material from the 1246 memorial, was organized into its present form sometime in the early fourteenth century. There is also a very early manuscript which was found in the library of Perugia (hence its name: the *Legenda Perugina)* that contains material from a number of sources including the *Vita Secunda* of Thomas of Celano. Scholars are sure that this manuscript does contain some of the material originally sent in by the three brothers and the British scholar Rosalind Brooke is sure that this legend is a redaction of the original memorial; she has recently published a bilingual Latin/ English edition of the *Legenda Perugina* with a most valuable introduction: *Scripta Leonis, Ruffini, et Angeli.*[21] The legend itself is of great importance because it witnesses independently to the source used by Thomas of Celano in writing the *Vita Secunda* and hence puts the whole Franciscan Question into some sort of clear focus.

If, as Rosalind Brooke and others believe, the *Legend of Perugia* does reflect rather faithfully the recollections of Brother Leo and the other early companions, the document is of inestimable value. It reflects recollections and conversations that come from those who were eyewitnesses and contemporaries of the saint. The document is characterized by its constant reporting of direct speech and although there is some obvious editorial work in these recollections, the ring of authenticity is there and, at times, the feeling that the authors have actually captured the cadence of the saint's conversation. The text is full of phrases that assure the reader that "we have seen this with our own eyes" or "often he would say to us" or "we heard him often remark" etc. John Moorman and others have analyzed the words and phrases of these "eyewitness" accounts and have identified certain recurrent themes and notions: the constant insistence of Saint Francis that the followers observe the Gospel in all of its rigor and to the letter; the way he would cause the friars to wonder due to his gift of prophecy; his insistence on the usages and customs of the brotherhood.[22] Rosalind Brooke has also noted that certain recurring phrases ("we have seen with our eyes"; the words *happiness* and *consolation)* give a sense of unity and continuity to the stories and argue to their essentially unified structure.[23]

The last spin-off of the original material sent in by the early friars is the *Speculum Perfectionis (The Mirror of Perfection).*[24] The manuscript was discovered in the last century by the great Franciscan scholar Paul Sabatier. At the time of its discovery Sabatier hailed it as the lost memorial of the three brothers (based, it turns out, on a misreading of the date on the *incipit* of the manuscript). Nearly one hundred years of research on Sabatier's manuscript (and a shorter version of it found in the Roman church of San Isadore) has shown that it is a fourteenth century compilation which has embedded in it some material that may have come from earlier testimony.

Since our present work is not historiographical but literary and cultural we cannot reconstruct more fully the intricate relationship that exists between these manuscript traditions. For our purposes it is sufficient to keep in mind the material that these ancient sources give us of the life of the saint and the scarcely concealed poignancy with which they describe the painful evolution of the order from its simple days of fraternity into the structured organization that the Franciscans eventually — perhaps, inevitably — became.

Two examples from these anonymous manuscripts might give some idea of the simple charm and ring of authenticity that may be found in these redactions. The stories are told both in the *Legend of Perugia* and the *Speculum Perfectionis*. Both came from the reminiscences of Brother Leo. The first is on poverty:

> Blessed Francis was seated near a fire and warming himself and this brother came and badgered him with the problem of his psalter. The saint answered him: "And when you have a psalter, you will want a breviary; and when you have breviary you will install yourself in a chair like a great prelate and you will order your brother: bring me my breviary!" As he said this he was carried away with great emotion, took some ashes from the hearth, sprinkled them on his head and rubbed some on himself repeating "That's my breviary!" The brother was completely dumbfounded and ashamed.[25]

The second selection deals with Saint Francis and his love for the natural world:

> We who lived with Saint Francis and who have written these memoirs bear witness that many times we heard him say: "If I could talk to the emperor, I would beg him, for the love of God, to grant my prayer and publish an edict forbidding anyone from trapping our sisters the larks or from inflicting any harm on them. Furthermore, all the podestas of the city, all the lords of the castles, and of the villages ought to oblige their subjects to throw wheat and grain on the road outside the cities and the towns so that on such a great feast the birds, and especially our sisters the larks, would have food . . . On Christmas day, finally, all the poor ought to be invited by the rich to a lavish meal."[26]

III   *The Writings of Bonaventure*

The biographies of Saint Francis written by Thomas of Celano and those that derived from his work and the memorials sent in by the three friars of Greccio did little to pacify or clarify the tumultuous positions that existed both within and outside the Franciscan Order. The *Vita Secunda* of Thomas of Celano gave the wing of the Franciscans much ammunition in their ongoing criticism of the Conventuals. The secular clergy, jealous of the mobility and the papal privileges given to the new mendicant orders (the Dominicans as well as the Franciscans), called into question the usefulness and even the legitimacy of the friars' manner of living. For all these reasons, the general chapter of the Franciscans that met in Narbonnes in 1260 looked for a new and definitive life of Saint Francis that would clearly set out the character of the life Francis, his message and his ideals, and his place in the mission of the church. The man who accepted the challenge of writing such a pacific work was none other than the general of the whole order, John Fidanza of Bagnoregio, better known to the world as Saint Bonaventure (died 1274), the greatest of the Franciscan theologians of the medieval period.

Bonaventure himself had not known Francis, as he himself admits in the prologue of his work, so he had to rely on firsthand interviews ("I went to his birthplace and visited the country where he lived and died. There I was able to speak with some of his close friends and to interview them carefully. . ."). Bonaventure also relied heavily on previous accounts already in circulation; in fact, he takes about seventy percent of his material directly from Thomas of Celano and then rewrites it according to his own needs and the exigencies of his own style. In the final analysis, very little of what Bonaventure wrote is new material; the only original stories that he produces are those dealing with the trip of Francis to Syria, probably from the accounts provided by Fra Illuminato (mentioned by name by Bonaventure) who had accompanied the saint to Damietta, and some few further details about the events surrounding the stigmata in 1224. Beyond that, Francis's new biographer relied on already published materials.

The *Legenda Major* does not, as Bonaventure reminds us in the prologue, follow chronological order, but rather a thematic order in which similar topics are grouped ". . .which happened at different times but concerned similar subjects while separating others which occurred at the same time but concerned different subjects." The *Legenda*, Bonaventure concludes, consists of fifteen chapters which treat systematically the following subjects: 1) his life in the world, 2) his conversion and the repair of churches in the environs of Assisi, 3) the foundation of his order and the first approval of the *Rule*, 4) the progress of order, 5) the austerity of his life, 6) his humility and his obedience, 7) his love of poverty, 8) his compassion, 9) his longing for martyrdom, 10) devotion to prayer, 11) his knowledge of Scripture and his intuition into the prophets, 12) preaching and his power of healing, 13) the stigmata, 14) his death, 15) canonization, and the translation of his remains to the basilica of Assisi. A final section then lists some of his posthumous miracles. It is thought (and some of the early manuscripts so state) that the work was so divided (i.e., into a prologue and fifteen chapters) so that the whole of the work could be read aloud to the friars during their meals on the feast of Saint Fran-

cis and for the seven days following, i.e., during the octave allowing
for two readings a day.

The portrait of Francis that emerges from Bonaventure's work is,
in the words of Bishop Moorman, "conventional and hagiogra-
phic."[27] Bonaventure's intention, after all, was to write a biography
in such a way as to avoid offense to any faction and to minimize the
elements in the story that would fuel further controversy either in or
outside the order. For that reason the extravagances of Francis are
skipped over, disputes within the order are underplayed, and sen-
sitive topics are skirted.

Bonaventure finished writing the *Legenda* around 1263[28] and over
thirty copies of it were made to be sent to the major provinces of the
order around the world. During this period Bonaventure also composed a condensed version of his work called the *Legenda Minor*.[29]
This condensation contained seven chapters subdivided into nine
"lessons" for each chapter. These "lessons" were for liturgical use,
i.e., they were read at the night Office of Matins during the octave of
the feast of Saint Francis. Bonaventure's work then had the official
approval of the order in that it was adopted both for liturgical and
extra-liturgical use within the Franciscan family. Because of this
acceptance and, presumably, because of the ambiguities contained
within the earlier works that favored the Spirituals, the general
chapter at Paris ordered the suppression of the earlier works on Francis, both inside the order and outside of it, thus making the *Legenda*
of Bonaventure the "official" life of the saint.

This draconian act of repression was rather systematically applied
and, as a result, few manuscript examples of the *Legendae* written
before Bonaventure have survived; many that did survive did so
because they were either in convents outside the Franciscan jurisdic-
tion or in convents hostile to the Conventuals. Yet these manuscripts
were little known to the larger public and it is safe to declare that
from the last third of the thirteenth century until the appearance of
the *Fioretti* the single most used source for the story of Francis was
the *Legenda Major* of Bonaventure. It was this version, for example,
that Dante utilized for all of his biographical information about the
saint. It has been said, for example, that those lines dealing with the
life of the saint in *Paradiso xi* are a poetic paraphrase of Bonaventure.

The most brilliant redoing of the *Legenda Major* of Bonaventure
is in the great series of frescos, long, but erroneously, attributed to
the hand of Giotto, that decorate the upper church of the basilica of

Saint Francis at Assisi. A brilliant and original study of these paintings done by the English scholar Alistair Smart shows that the whole of the iconographical program of the cycle is based on a theological reading of the *Legenda Major*.[30] That Bonaventure's *Legenda* is the primary source for this cycle on the life of Francis is first proved because originally there were painted titles taken from Bonaventure's text[31] under each of the paintings. It is Smart's theory that each of the panels must be read in more than a biographical sense. The animator of the whole series (usually now referred to as the "Master of the Saint Francis cycle") was not primarily interested in simply telling of the life of the saint based on incidents representative of his life but rather was interested in making the doctrinal point that Saint Francis was, as Bonaventure states in the prologue, an *alter christus*—another Christ: ". . . the central declaration of the glory of Saint Francis, as one raised with Christ and exalted to a heavenly throne among the angels."[32]

According to Smart, the fresco cycle should be "read" as if it contained seven chapters. The first three scenes are a prelude to the active ministry of Francis; they point to and prophesy about his future ministry. The second "chapter" reveals Francis as the destined savior of the church; this section culminates in the dream of Pope Innocent III who sees a figure in brown propping up the tottering cathedral of Saint John Lateran. The third "chapter" relates prophetic moments about the coming glory of Francis and of the rewards given to him as a result of his humility. Scene four tells of the success of his ministry and its final seal of approval, i.e., the stigmata. The fifth section deals with the death of Francis and his reception into heaven, while the sixth ties into the fifth as it narrates the funeral of Francis, his canonization, and subsequent apparition to Pope Gregory IX. The last section of the cycle, faithful to the literary structure of most of the *Legendae*, "proves" the glory of Francis, and his power, by narrating some of his posthumous miracles. This great fresco cycle, one of the greatest artistic monuments of the Western world, bears eloquent witness to the influence of Bonaventure's work and, in the words of Smart, "One of the miracles of the Assisi cycle is the perfect manner in which the pictorial language expresses the sublime themes expounded in the *Legenda Major*."[33]

The *Legenda* was also the probable source of the Franciscan cycle done by Giotto in the Bardi chapel of the chapel of Santa Croce in

Florence sometime after 1317. The scenes in this Franciscan cycle include only the following: Francis and his father before the bishop of Assisi; the vision of Francis at Arles; the death of Francis; the presentation of the *Rule* to Pope Innocent III; Francis preaching before the Sultan at Damietta; and the stigmata. These scenes were obviously drawn from the *Legenda Major* since the scene showing Francis willing to undergo the trail by fire before the sultan is found only in Bonaventure even though it is repeated in the *Fioretti* which was written after this cycle was completed. Finally, the *Legenda Major* was more than likely the source and inspiration for the fresco cycle done by Gozzoli at the church of San Francisco at Montefalco during the fifteenth century, although the figure of Francisco himself, enshrined in a mandala, was also probably inspired by some of the Joachimite tendencies of the Spiritual Franciscans.[34]

Beside the two biographical works of the *Legenda Major* and the *Legenda Minor* it should also be noted that in the vast output of his literary career, Bonaventure turned again and again to the life of Francis in sermons on the life of the saint and in various mystical writings.[35] The most important of these later works is the Latin mystical treatise *Itinerarium Mentis ad Deum (Journey of the Mind to God)*.[36] In the introduction to that work Bonaventure wrote that he went to La Verna, the site of the stigmata of Francis, "Thirty three years after his death" (i.e., in 1259 - 60) and that there he wrote the *Itinerarium* as a result of his contemplation of the stigmata of the saint. This work, one of the authentic masterpieces of medieval mysticism, describes six steps (mystically derived from the six-winged seraph that Francis saw in his vision at La Verna) that lead men to God: two steps outside of men; two within men (reason and grace); and two above men, namely, the contemplation of God in His essence and in His trinitarian manifestation. The first two steps to God are based on a contemplation of the natural world around us. This reflection is a philosophical refinement of the lyric statement of the *Canticle of Brother Sun* that every creature in the created world is redolent (*porta significazione*) of the most high Creator (*dell'Altissimo*). In the final section of the *Itinerarium* Bonaventure writes of the ecstasy of the contemplation of God in a passage of lyrical, and typically Franciscan, intensity: "We die, then, and we enter into mystery. We impose silence on our cares, our drives, and our dreams. With Christ crucified we leave this world for the Father, and having seen Him, we say with Phillip 'it is enough';

we hear Saint Paul 'your grace suffices' and with David: 'My flesh and heart weaken. God of my heart—my portion is God forever. May the Lord be eternally blest. All the people will say. Amen. Amen."

IV *The* Fioretti

At the conclusion of a very informative paper on Saint Francis and popular piety, Professor E. Delaruelle wrote that the greatest accomplishment of Francis was that he proved capable of overcoming the tension that exists between two diverse currents of Christianity; the one, clerical, esoteric, inaccessible to the crowd; the other, simple, at the margin of doctrinal formulations, filled with the spirit of the *naif*.[37] Because of this balance, Delaruelle concludes, the portraits that emerge from the *Legenda Major* of Saint Bonaventure and the *Fioretti* should not be as contradictory but as complementary.

It is the *Fioretti* that has captured the imagination of modern man and it is to that book that men so naturally turn when they wish to read about the saint. So completely is the *Fioretti* identified that some have thought that it came from the pen of the saint himself. The work has been translated into all of the modern languages[38] and it has been a source for much art of Franciscan inspiration. The present writer, for instance, remembers with intense pleasure an outdoor performance of some scenes of the *Fioretti* done by the *piccolo teatro* of Milan using the grand Romanesque facade of San Miniato al Monte in Florence as a stagedrop. Iris Origo in her great book on quattrocento Tuscany, *The Merchant of Prato*, recounts how the *Fioretti* was favorite nighttime reading for Tuscan worthies of the day and how fathers read it aloud to their children in the evening as a sort of bedtime story.[39] No wonder that the *Fioretti* has been called the "breviary of the Italian people." Yet this charming collection of stories, written in limpid Tuscan dialect, has a tortured history from a literary point of view and was born out of intense and bitter struggles within the Franciscan family.

In 1902 Paul Sabatier discovered a Latin manuscript entitled *Actus Beati Francisci et Sociorum Ejus;* a few years later the English scholar A. G. Little discovered a better version of the same manuscript. This Latin *Actus* seems to be the source of the Italian *Fioretti*. The *Actus* appears to be the work of a Brother Ugolino who names himself several times in the text. Scholars debate as to whether this Ugolino is Ugolino da Brunforte or Ugolino da

Boniscambi, the former dying about 1300, the latter about 1340. At any rate, Brother Ugolino relates a whole series of stories about Saint Francis that had been told to him by Brother Jacopo della Massa; this friar, in turn, had been an intimate friend of Brother Leo, the confidant and secretary of the saint. The *Actus* then reflects a second generation of oral tradition about the saint: Brother Leo sharing his reminiscences with Jacopo della Massa who relates them to Ugolino, author of the *Actus*. The second half of the *Actus* relates stories, not of the saint, but of certain holy friars who lived in the Marches around Ancona in the northern part of Italy—an area filled with small convents and hermitages of friars very close to the Spiritualist tradition whose life was one of extreme poverty, retreat from the world, and intensive contemplation.

Some fifty years after the writing of the *Actus* and its circulation, an unknown friar from Tuscany selected fifty-two chapters from the *Actus* and translated them into Italian. To these chapters he added a section, composed by himself, entitled "Five Considerations on the Stigmata" using previously circulated sources such as the *Actus* itself, the *Lives* of Celano and Bonaventure, and others. The original *Fioretti* (some later manuscripts have tacked on all sorts of miscellaneous chapters) contained thirty-seven chapters on the life of Saint Francis and his early friars; five chapters on events and miracles in the life of Saint Anthony of Padua; and ten chapters that recount stories of the pious friars of the Marches of Ancona. After these chapters are the "Five Considerations on the Stigmata."[40]

The title of this work—*I Fioretti di San Francesco*—literally means "The Little Flowers." We remember that in their 1246 letter to the general of the order of Saint Francis, the three friars of Greccio appended a letter to their memorial saying that their intention was "to gather the most beautiful flowers of the many blooming in a pleasant field" and that they "did not propose to follow an historical sequence."[41] Yet we should have a clear idea of what the bouquet of flowers meant to a medieval audience. To our ears the title sounds piously romantic but in the usage of the time, as Edmund Gardner has noted, *fioretti* simply meant an anthology of stories or a compilation without respect to historical sequence.[42] The words of Serge Hughes are germane at this point: "It would be good, then, if on rereading the *Fioretti* we could restrain our pre-Raphaelite tendencies and our inclinations towards pastel reminiscences."[43] There is, after all, little of the "pastel" in the bitter polemics found in some of the pages of the *Fioretti*. It contains not only spirited defenses of ab-

solute poverty but direct attacks on illustrious figures in the order
who seemed to have betrayed the ideals of the saint. Brother Elias,
the successor to the saint as head of the order and a favorite *bête
noire* of the Spirituals, is depicted as being snatched from damnation
only at the end of his life through the merciful intercession of the
saint. Saint Bonaventure himself is described as a clawed monster
who would have torn away at the "true" friars had Christ himself not
sent Francis to blunt his sharp talons.

Yet, polemics aside, it is in the *Fioretti* that some of the most
beautiful and best remembered of the legends about the saint are
preserved: Saint Francis "converting" the fierce wolf of Gubbio into
the gentle "Brother Wolf" who placidly walked the city streets until
he died of old age; the conversation of Clare and Francis on the love
of God that reached such an intensity the people of Assisi thought
the convent was on fire; Saint Francis explaining to Brother Leo the
meaning of perfect joy; Francis and Ruffino preaching naked
through the streets of Assisi; Francis preaching to the birds; the encounter of Francis and the prostitute while he travelled in the Middle East; the bread and water meal of the friars, served on a flat rock,
which Francis insisted was a sumptuous meal. All of these stories
have passed into the folklore, not only of Italy, but of the entire
Christian West and have been largely responsible for the shaping of
the *persona* of the saint. Indeed, it could be argued, that the
rediscovery of the *Fioretti* in the last century and its acceptance as
the authentic text of the Franciscan ideal by the non-expert has
largely contributed to the romanticization of the saint in the popular
imagination. By a selective reading of the *Fioretti* (little attention is
paid to the section of the *Fioretti* on the stigmata) the modern age
had tended to cast Francis in the role of the gentle animal-lover who
practiced the most attractive of the virtues of Christianity. The text
of the *Fioretti* permits such a superficial reading since it is written in
a limpid Italian with little of the heavy-handed sermonizing that one
associates with the works of Celano and Bonaventure.

The *Fioretti* is also valuable as a collection because its second part,
consisting of stories and anecdotes of the holy friars of the Marches,
does give us some clear idea of how the ideals of Francis could go
away, not in the direction of laxity, but in the direction of unreflec-
tive slavishness. In this section of the book, as Serge Hughes has
said, the simplicity of Francis gives way to the simplism of his
followers. The anti-intellectualism of Francis (undoubtedly present
in his own philosophy of life) gives way to pure obscurantism. The

poetic acts of simplicity that mark the life of Francis are distorted into foolishness and humorless acts of fanaticism by some of the friars of the Marches. These stories are instructive if for no other reason than to hold in check any tendency to overromanticize the Spirituals, beleaguered though they may have been. As Rapheal Brown so wryly notes, Brother Juniper, one of these legendary holy men, was a perfect example of a friar in dire need of expert and firm spiritual direction.[44]

A final question remains: how historical are the stories found in the *Fioretti*? Even a cursory reading of the stories shows that they have been embellished and exaggerated for the purpose of edification. Yet a direct oral tradition links the author of the *Actus* (the source of the *Fioretti*) back to the early companions of Francis through the reminiscences of Brother Jacopo of Massa. A detailed historical analysis of all of the stories has not been done yet but many scholars are convinced that many of them have an historical kernel and that no biography of the saint would be complete without a judicious use of this source.[45]

In the last analysis, however, it is not for their historical worthiness but for their poetic charm that the *Fioretti* are read. One can ask what the poetic quality is that makes the *Fioretti* so readable and so endearing to so many people even in our own day. Arturo Pompeati thinks that the *Fioretti* have that quality by which Franciscan spirituality is kept to the earth, i.e., to the realm of our experience, but with a certain luminosity and lightness that tend to deny the heaviness and the weight of human existence.[46] The style of the Italian manages to convey at one and the same time a sense of this world (especially in the use of vivid and immediate images that fly right to the imagination) while not holding us to it. There is a sense both of the texture of sensual beauty and the need for the ascetic moment. If one were given to oxymoronic speech, the term "earthy unearthliness" might be the phrase to use to catch the spirit of the *Fioretti*'s style.

This simplicity and limpidity is not only conveyed by the style and tone but also by the emphases in the stories: the praise of humility; the hymn to the goodness and sacramentality of God's creation; the search for perfect joy; the happiness to be found in the search for simplicity and humility. In short, the *Fioretti* attempt to search out the infancy of the soul, simple and clean from baptism and free from the stain of life. It is, to borrow a phrase from Professor Getto, a "fable of Christian perfection."[47]

Undergirding this ideal of Christian perfection are sharply etched stories that show the possibility that every person, no matter his state or position, is capable of receiving the divine largesse. The *Fioretti* contains no heavy moralizing; there are either sharply drawn moral lessons or equally pointed stories about the possibility of salvation: God comes to aid the demon-tortured Fra Ruffino; the Sultan is saved on his deathbed; Brother Elias is a recipient of deathbed conversion; even the evil wolf of Gubbio is not beyond the graciousness of God through the hands of the saint. That mixture of charm, hope, and limpid purity has drawn people to the *Fioretti* throughout the years, despite its childlike qualities—or, perhaps, because of them.

V *The Early Franciscan Chronicles*

This chapter would not be complete without some rapid mention of the earliest chronicles written by Franciscans in the years after the death of the saint. We have, so as not to go too far afield, restricted our consideration of those chronicles to those written in the thirteenth century, i.e., the century of the death of the saint. We mention these chronicles for two reasons. In the first place, at least one of the writers knew Saint Francis personally and thus providesl us with a few reminiscences of the saint. Secondly, we have already seen how contentious life was in the early Franciscan Order; these chronicles give us a better picture of the spread of the friars to the other parts of the Christian world and give us some sense of the daily life of the friars and the vicissitudes of their life both within and without the order in its most formative and definitive years.

The *Chronicle* of Brother Jordan of Giano *(Chronica Fratris Jordani a Iano OFM)*[48] was, in the words of the author, dictated to a certain Brother Baldwin of Brandenburg ("I doing the narrating and Brother Baldwin the writing") while the two of them were at the Franciscan convent of Halberstadt, Germany, in April of 1262. Jordan was from the village of Giano near Spoleto and was born around 1195. According to a later chronicler, Jordan was received into the Franciscans by Saint Francis. It is presumed that this must have been in 1219 before Saint Francis went to the Orient. Jordan was already a deacon and was later ordained to the priesthood. In 1221 he was sent as a part of a mission band to Germany and, with the exception of two trips to Italy in 1230 and 1238, he lived and worked in various parts of Germany. He held various offices in Germany and was vicar of the Franciscans in Poland and Bohemia. After 1242, when he was elected vicar of Saxony, we do not hear of him again until he writes in 1262. We presume that he died shortly thereafter but the date of his death and the place of his burial remain uncertain.

The present text of the *Chronicle* is not entirely complete. We possess sixty-two chapters that are surely from the hand of Jordan; another series that is often called the *Continuatio Saxonica* (that may be from another pen); and three letters describing the invasions of the Mongols in Eastern Europe — these almost certainly from the pen of Jordan. The present *Chronicle* then contains: a prologue; seventy-eight chapters and the three letters of Jordan. The chapters are very short and range from a discussion of matters that happened in Italy prior to Jordan's trip to Germany, the growth of the order in Germany itself, and, finally, the Saxon material and the three letters on the Mongols.[49]

For our present purposes the first chapters are of most importance because they provide another window into the life of the saint and the dealings of his order in some of its most crucial years, 1219 to 1221. He wrote these accounts many years after the events described but with few lapses, some of which he himself was aware of (he could not remember the year when the friars were martyred in the East, for example). In fact, alone among the early historians, he gives a relatively straightforward account of the difficulties in the order during the years 1919 - 21 and is also frank and informative about the decline of the famous (or, infamous) Brother Elias.

Jordan does not spend much time on the early life of Saint Francis since "enough has been said in the *Legenda* about how his conversion took place . . . " (1). Jordan describes the early mission of the friars who had been sent both to France and to Germany, including their trials because of their ignorance of the language: in France they were taken for Albigensians; in Germany for Lombard heretics; in Hungary people set dogs on them. Jordan goes on to recount in the briefest manner the trip of Francis to Morocco, his return, and the troubles in the order; the granting of a protector in the person of Cardinal Hugolin of Ostia; the chapters of 1219 and 1221 (where he gets somewhat confused in the separation of incidents in these chapters); and, finally, (17 - 18) the sending of the mission to Germany and Jordan's own inclusion in that number. From that point on Jordan is really dealing with the early history of the friars in Germany and although that account is fascinating in its own right and important as an historical document, it is, nonetheless, outside the purview of this discussion.

The *Chronicle* of Brother Jordan is written in fairly good Latin with an occasional turn of phrase that betrays the Italian origin of the author. He says of himself that he was not learned and he makes no attempt to reach for elegance in his latinity. But, for all that, there is a certain vigor in the *Chronicle* (and it is blessedly free of the lengthy digression and *catenae* of scriptural texts which Salimbene loved so much). One must agree with the judgment of Father Placid Hermann:

> It is therefore necessary to recognize this as a document of great importance. The sense of humor of its author makes the chronicle agreeable and easy reading matter. The narrative, vigorous as it is in its historical exactitude, is presented in a pleasing way. But Brother Jordan knows how to be moving too, and, when he tells us about Saint Francis and about the memory of him among the brethren, he creates terms that are discreetly moving and we can understand the place the saintly founder of the Order held in the hearts of his brethren who knew him personally.[50]

There are four manuscripts conserved in England (two in the British Museum, one at the cathedral library of York, and the Phillips manuscript of Cheltenham) that recount the early history of the Franciscan Order in England from about 1229 until about 1258 — that is, from its beginnings until about the time of Brother Adam Marsh. These manuscripts have been used as the basis for the text of the chronicle edited by the famous Franciscanists A. G. Little and John Moorman: *Fratris Thomae, vulgo dicti de Eccleston Tractatus De Adventu Fratrum Minorum in Angliam (A Treatise on the Coming of the Friars Minor to England by Brother Thomas surnamed Eccleston).*[51]

Of this Brother Thomas we know extremely little, even his surname only coming to us courtesy of a title page from a seventeenth century manuscript. From the chronicle itself we learn only that he entered the order sometime between 1229 and 1232; that he had studied at Oxford and that he probably lived for some time at a convent in London. He uses some curial language and some have inferred from this that he had had some legal training (at Oxford?) and that he may have been ordained to the priesthood, but that is not clearly stated in the text. The chronicle is dedicated to a Brother Simon of Ashby but, again, of this person nothing is known though it is surmised that he was a superior of a Franciscan house.

The chronicle itself (at least as reflected in the various manuscripts) is not at all well organized and the Latin, while better than that of Brother Jordan of Giano, is, as Placid Hermann kindly puts it, not "a model for imitation."[52] The actual information about Saint Francis himself is very slight though there is this shining testimony that Brother Thomas records from the testimony of another brother:

Incident. Brother John of Parma, the minister general, in the full chapter at Genoa ordered Brother Bonitius, who had been a companion of Saint Francis to tell the brothers the truth about the stigmata of the saint, because many in the world were doubting this matter. And he replied with tears: 'These sinful eyes have seen them; and these sinful hands have touched them.'[53]

A few scraps of testimony about the stigmata of Saint Francis on La Verna are interesting; the incident of the anointing of the rock is not recorded elsewhere:

But Brother Leo, the companion of Saint Francis, told Brother Peter, the minister of England, that the apparition of the Seraphim came to Saint Francis while was wrapt up in contemplation and more clearly even than was written in his life, and that many things were revealed to him that he did not communicate to any living person. But he did tell Brother Rufinus, his companion, that when he saw the angel from afar, he was greatly afraid, and that the angel treated him harshly; and he told him that his Order would continue to the end of the world, that no one who hated the Order would live long, that no one evil would remain long in the Order, and that no one who truly loved the Order would come to a bad end. But Saint Francis commanded Brother Rufinus to wash and anoint with oil the stone on which the angel had stood; this he did. These things Brother Warin of Sedenefeld wrote down from the lips of Brother Leo.[54]

If the Chronicle of Brother Thomas of Eccleston is short on details about the life of the saint there is one facet of the chronicle that should engage our attention. The major part of the chronicle is devoted to a description of the various foundations of Franciscans in England and their progress. This is beyond our purview but incidental hints in the text suggest how the friars were coming to grips with the observance of poverty and the burgeoning growth of the order; random statements and observations of Brother Thomas give us some hints as to how the friars were handling the much-disputed question of evangelical poverty as it was reflected both in the Franciscan legislation and in the disputes of the day. Here are some random samples:

Brother Thomas exalted poverty first by telling edifying anecdotes about the superiors and their love for this distinctive virtue; a small sampling of these incidents should give an idea of their general tenor:
Brother Albert said that three things especially have exalted our Order, namely, the bare feet, the poor quality of our clothing, and the rejection of money.
He [Brother Haymo] was so zealous for poverty that in a provincial chapter he sat with the brothers upon the ground in the refectory, clothed in a very worn and torn habit.

But besides these pious stories there are other indications about the concept and practice of poverty. Cap. x of the chronicle treats of the buildings and friaries that the friars were accumulating in England. We see in this chapter a certain tension: the necessity of having places and the attendant fear that in their acquisition a weakening of poverty and a heightening of avarice were being experienced. We find in that chapter, for example, discussions on the question of mud walls versus stone walls as befitting the feel for poverty; the request of Brother Haymo (later a general of the whole order) that the brothers acquire ample lands so that they could cultivate rather than beg for their food; reproofs to brothers who were over-zealous in the collecting of alms for the good of the brothers ("Brother William, you used to speak so spiritually; but now your whole speech is: give, give, give!"); dreams in which Saint Francis appeared to order the destruction of overly elaborate buildings, one of which actually collapsed before the brothers would take up their residence and their finding some verses in the rubble: "God's grace doth teach us by this very ruin/That man should be content with smaller houses."

Both Brother Jordan and Brother Thomas seem to have been model Franciscans of the early stamp: pious, credulous, zealous for the life of poverty, and deeply attached to the memory of Saint Francis. The third chronicler who deserves some mention in this section is far more cast in the mold of Chaucer's friar: witty, very gossipy, slightly addicted to the pleasure of the grape, not above a pretty girl's glance, and somewhat detached from the more austere preoccupations of medieval mendicant friars. Such a man was Fra Salimbene, a curious mixture of genuine piety, some learning, and not a little *joie de vivre*. His lengthy chronicle is least important for our understanding of Saint Francis (he barely mentions him at all) but is worthy of at least some mention because of the vast amount of incidental information that it provides on the times in which he lived.[55]

Salimbene was born in Parma in 1221; his family name was Ognibene (i.e., "all-good") but when he was received into the order in 1238 his name was changed to Salimbene (i.e., "rise to good") on the grounds that God alone was to be called "All good." Salimbene lived in various parts of Italy until after his ordination to the deaconate in 1246; in 1247 he was sent to study in Paris but evidently lasted only one week there, leaving to make two long journeys through France in the following two years. He was in Genoa in 1249 where he was ordained to the priesthood and for the rest of his life he lived, without particularly distinguishing himself in the order, in various parts of Italy. The chronicle that he has left mentions him as being at various times domiciled in Bologna, Forlì, Parma, Imola, Reggio, Faenza, Ravenna, Ferrara, etc.

Only one text of Salimbene's chronicle exists and it is thought to be an autograph. It is preserved in the Vatican Library and parts of it are missing. It seems that Salimbene not only wished to chronicle his own observations, travels, and adventures, but also intended, with the panache so characteristic of the period, to chronicle the world's history. His own manuscript contains the chronicles of others that he copied wholesale, reflections on history, long-ranging digressions on matters containing Sacred Scripture together with copius excerpts from the same, descriptions of his two voyages to France, a fair share of immodest stories somewhat after the pungent style of Boccaccio, and his own reflections about the things that he has seen. In fact, as Placid Hermann has noted, this seems to be one of the great merits of the chronicles since "they give us the intimate and spontaneous sentiments of an historian contemporary with the facts that he relates."[56] But, as Hermann goes on to note, Salimbene often gets swamped with the trivial at the expense of events that were of great historical significance: thus, in 1282 he tells us that there were so many caterpillars in the trees that they lost all of their leaves, but has no note of the famous massacre at Palermo known to historians and opera buffs as *Il Vespri Siciliani* — the Sicilian Vespers.

For all that, Salimbene's chronicle is important for the incidental information that he gives us on a wide range of interesting topics from the great penitential march of 1260 (already discussed in the previous chapter) to the status of the early friars in France. Salimbene is, by turns, wordy and pungent but his chronicle for all of its lack has been an important source for the serious historian who wished to get a clearer picture of thirteenth century France, a France that was as important for the great university of Paris (which Salimbene describes) as for the papal court at Lyons. It is not an unimportant piece of documentation for the total picture of the early Franciscan movement.

CHAPTER 4

The Franciscan Revival of Modern Times

THE great flowering of Franciscan literature ended in a sense with the *Fioretti*. Although the Franciscans continued to give great service to the Church and to the world with their pens and their activities, interest in the saint and his ideas lessened outside the pale of institutional Catholicism. Franciscans contributed little to the leading ideas of the Renaissance and, except for the reform movements of the Franciscan-inspired Capuchins, had little original impact on the Counter Reformation, that movement being mainly inspired by the genius of the Jesuits. In the period of the Enlightenment not only was there no interest in the ideas of the Franciscans but there was a good deal of overt hostility. The gibe of Voltaire could well stand for the general attitude of the Enlightenment and post-Enlightenment intelligentsia: "I am not overly pleased with that man Francis, who thought a real Christian should go begging in the street, and wanted his sons, those robust lazybones, to take an oath to live at our expense."[1] We have already noted that Goethe found little to interest him in Assisi outside the Roman temple that stood in its main square. Within the limited scope of this study it is not possible to chart the decline of the Franciscan spirit and influence after its great flowering in the thirteenth and fourteenth centuries nor is that decline absolute since Franciscan impulses still had a good deal of influence on popular piety while the Franciscan school of philosophy (Scotus and Occam) had a profound influence on late medieval theology. One aspect of this decline might give some idea of the changing ideas and the waning of the Franciscan influence on European culture as it moved from the late medieval to the Renaissance period in Italy. In a very instructive study published in 1938, Hans Baron has demonstrated that the Franciscan emphasis on poverty had powerful resonances in the writings of the fourteenth century humanists.[2] These humanists were quite concerned with the

109

qualities necessary for men to live the good life, i.e., the life devoted to humanist ideals. Baron has shown that many of the early humanists insisted that a detachment from worldly wealth and honors (a detachment that was inspired largely by reason of the Franciscan presence) was a *sine qua non* of the scholarly and humanistic life: the watchword of this idea was supplied by Brunetto Latini in the *Tresor* (1265): "Diogenes in his poverty was richer than Alexander in his greatness."[3] Dante inveighed against the "new" Florence with its love of riches and its spirit of materialism and contrasted this new Florence with the sober and parsimonious Florence of old. Again, in the *Paradiso* Dante hymned Francis as the representative of poverty and praised him as an exemplar. Petrarch wrote throughout his life about the concept of *mediocritas* (that wealth sufficient for life but not excessive or inordinate) and attempted sporadically to live personally in possession of few things and without what we would call today "conspicuous consumption"; his retreat at Vaucluse being a symbol of this desire for the simple life.

In the fifteenth century, Baron has written, this attitude was changing and the change was especially noticeable in the works of humanist writers of the city of Florence such as Bruni, Landino, and Alberti. There was an insistence that the goods of the body were needed in order to provide for the good of the soul. Funeral panegyrics composed and delivered by the humanists at the funerals of the wealthy lauded the deceased for the acquisition of money and wealth and the use of these possessions for the enhancement of the cultural and civic life of the city. Also the laity was becoming more aware of their own place in the scheme of the social life of the church and felt that their contribution must arise from the arena of life in the world. In short, as social and economic life became more developed and rationalized, there was less patience with the world-denying asceticism of the friars and their philosophy of otherworldliness; Marvin Becker makes the point well:

. . . the broader community could no longer be supported by the restricted allegiances of the past; institutions of the commune such as the guilds and the *Parte Guelfa* were too parochial. Feeling for one's city and fellows required contempt for those hypocritical friars preaching the doctrine of voluntary poverty. Underlying humanist polemics against monasticism was the implicit rejection of any claims that the clergy held a monopoly on God's sacred manna. Neither Poggio nor Lorenzo Valla denied the value of monastic institutions, but they did attack any denigration of the spiritual prerogatives of the laity. Firm endorsement of the dignity of the secular odyssey sometimes encouraged an invidious, ironic comparision between monk and layman. The former, it would seem, took the easier path towards salvation living under the vows, while the latter selected the hard road while remaining in the world of temptation . . . In securing the spiritual dignity of the laic role, Bruni, Poggio, and Valla also contended that contempt for honest work and praise of mendacity destroyed the very fabric of civilization. Indeed, those lofty eras of world history, had frequently been times of great civic wealth. The intentions of many humanist polemics against monastic targets were to enhance the possibility of realizing a "true" Christian community where affluent citizens would be fully cognizant of their social responsibilities.[4]

The secular rejection of the Franciscan ideal is epitomized by the attitude of Machiavelli who stands at the end of the great days of the Florentine Renaissance. In Book III, chapter 1 of the *Discourses* (on Livy) Machiavelli discusses religion and notes that all sectarian movements that have had any longevity depended, for that longevity, on the ability of the sect to go back to its original principles and renew itself in terms of those pristine ideas. Machiavelli then goes on to say that in the thirteenth century the reform movements of Saint Francis and Saint Dominic were able to energize and renew an essentially moribund and stagnating Christianity. The interesting point is that Machiavelli was not pleased with their effort despite his admiration for the purity and zeal of the two men involved. Unlike Dante who saw the founders of the mendicant movements as the epitome of Christianity and as authentic exemplars of all that was noble, Machiavelli was forced to condemn the two men and point them out as sustainers of the rottenness of the body politic. Machiavelli was unhappy with the very success of their evangelical reform since, by preaching a doctrine of submission to authority and holding out a hope for reward in the next life, these reformers kept people both from realizing the basic injustices of the ruling class and the possibility of renewing the political order. Machiavelli sets up a dichotomy between those who accepted the otherworldly teaching of Christianity that came from the friars and those who exercised power without either a belief in Christianity or in the possibility of punishment in the next life; thus, these rulers, both secular and ecclesiastical, were able to do their worst to a people who had been taught to suffer for the sake of heaven.

In short, the teaching of Francis and his friars permitted the worst kind of tyranny to run rampant (*e così quegli fanno il peggio che possono, perchè non temono quella punizione che non veggono e non credono*).[5] Unlike the praise of the possibility of humanization and divinization inherent in the evangelical truth of Christianity taught by Dante, Machiavelli sees Christianity as essentially a debilitating religion. Machiavelli is a precursor of an attitude that would be closely articulated by thinkers as diverse as Edward Gibbon, Karl Marx, and the Victorian poet Algernon Swinburne. Joseph Mazzeo sums up Machiavelli's position succinctly: "Christianity teaches humility and submission, an other worldly goal, and a contempt for worldly ones; whereas paganism taught men to cultivate greatness of soul, the classical *magnanimitas*, and strength of body, values which served to make men formidable. The result of belief in Christianity has been to make men feeble, a prey to evil minded men who can through its use more easily control the kind of people who believe they gain heaven by enduring injustice."[6]

It was in the nineteenth century, largely under the influence of Romanticism and Neo-Medievalism, that interest in Saint Francis was rekindled. Omer Englebert, in a survey of that period, has shown how writers such as Stendhal, Chateaubriand, Michelet, Taine, and Goerres began to emphasize the lyrical qualities of the Franciscan period.[7] In 1849 the French critic Antoine Ozanam published his *Les Poetes Franciscans* in which he spoke of Francis as the fountainhead of serious vernacular poetry in the Christian West. In Germany, Henry Thode published *Franz von Assisi und Die Anfänge der Kunst in Italien* (Berlin, 1885), a book which argues that the new art of the Italian Renaissance had its original impetus in the Franciscan movement as a whole. Most of the works written in this period, like those of Ozanam and Thode, emphasized the simplicity of the life of Francis, its "poetic and lyrical" quality, his love of nature, and the nonecclesiastical cast of his life style. Yet it was not only a romantic revival and a sense of the beauty of the culture of the medieval period that inspired these people; there was also the desire to deepen the common knowledge of the historical periods of that time and to reevaluate the whole medieval period in relation to the Renaissance. Thode's book was written explicitly for this purpose.

Henry Thode's *Franz von Assisi* was essentially an answer and a challenge to the central thesis of Jacob Burckhardt's influential *The Civilization of the Renaissance in Italy (Die Cultur der Renaissance in Italien* — 1860). Burckhardt's book, still the *point du départ* in Renaissance historiography, argued that the rise of individualism, brought about through a new understanding of statecraft, a complexification of the Italian economic picture, and a revitalized study of ancient learning and culture resulted in the era that we know as the Renaissance. Burckhardt, or at least those who have followed Burckhardt over the years, saw Renaissance man emerge as an almost titanic creature, sure of himself and centered in his own world rather than under the theocratic umbrella of medieval culture. For Burckhardt this came about because of the recovery of the classical understanding of the individual. Thode's book takes issue with Burckhardt precisely at this point. For Thode, the individualism of the Renaissance and the renewed interest in nature and its reconciliation with religion came not because of a study of Roman antiquity but because of the religious mysticism and the subjective energy of the Middle Ages. As Wallace Ferguson has noted, Thode saw Saint Francis of Assisi as both the culmination of the medieval religious experience and the first inspiration for the emergence of Renaissance culture.[8] Thode argued that it was from Saint Francis and his religious revival that this spirit arose. Indeed, it is a thesis of Thode's work that there is a direct, if subtle, line running from the Franciscan revival through humanism, right down to the Protestant Reformation.

Thode's book did not have an immediate impact on the mainlines of Renaissance interpretation at the time of its publication; Burckhardt still held the field. Yet the Thode thesis received new attention with the publication of Sabatier's biography of Saint Francis (to be discussed later on) and the worldwide attention that the biography received. Sabatier's biography of Saint Francis reinforced Thode's conception of Saint Francis and, in the process, gave impetus to a serious interest in the study of the religious sources and currents that undergird the whole phenomenon of the Renaissance.[9]

Yet the interest in Saint Francis was not confined to those scholars such as Sabatier and Thode who were interested in Saint Francis from the historical viewpoint. The rediscovery of the medieval period brought renewed interest in the saint to writers who were neither antiquarians nor academic scholars. Matthew Arnold, the English poet and critic, may be seen as representative of these nineteenth century admirers of Saint Francis. Arnold had spent a good deal of his literary life struggling over the problems of religion and culture and was vividly aware of the tensions between the two. In the life of Saint Francis he was able to perceive and appreciate the fusion of the religious and the poetic spirit:

The beginnings of the mundane poetry of the Italians are in Sicily, at the court of kings; the beginnings of their religious poetry are in Umbria, with Saint Francis. His are the upper humble waters of a mighty stream; at the beginning of the thirteenth century it is Saint Francis, at the end, Dante. Now it happens that Saint Francis, too, like the Alexandrian songstress, has his hymn for the sun, our Adonis. *Canticle of the Sun, Canticle of the Creatures* — the poem goes by both names. Like the Alexandrian hymn, it is designed for popular use, but not for use by King Ptolemy's people; artless in language, irregular in rhythm, it matches with the childlike genuis that produced it, and the simple natures that loved and repeated . . ."[10]

The central figure in the revival of Franciscan studies was the Protestant theologian and pastor, Paul Sabatier. Sabatier had been a student of the noted scholar Ernest Renan at the *College de France* and it was Renan who encouraged Sabatier to pursue a study of the saint of Assisi. Later in his life Sabatier recalled that in 1884 Renan told him when he was still a student that he should do such a thorough studv in order to rehabilitate the saint in European estimation: "And you [Sabatier], you shall be the historian of the Seraphic Father. I envy you. Saint Francis has always smiled on his historians. He saved the Church in the thirteenth century, and ever since then his spirit has remained strangely alive. We need him. If we really want him, he will come back . . ."[11]

Accepting Renan's challenge, Sabatier published his *Vie de St. Francois* in 1894 after some years of intensive research into the early Franciscan sources, research that he would continue with great fruit until the end of his life. The book was an immediate success and not only went through many editions but was republished in the major European languages. Sabatier's biography had a number of qualities that virtually insured it a permanent place in Franciscan literature. Published at the end of the nineteenth century when interest in Saint Francis had already matured over the years, Sabatier's book was the end result of serious scholarship and intimate familiarity with the sources. He was able to remove Saint Francis from the strict confines of the Roman Catholic hagiographical tradition and put the claims of Francis before a wider, and less orthodox, audience.

More importantly, Sabatier's book was not only a chronological biography but an interpretative (we are almost tempted to say, polemical) one. The basic thesis of Sabatier was that Saint Francis had been a lay mystic who had wished to live a life of simple evangelical poverty as a living contrast to the landbound, hieratic, and overly structured institutions of monasticism, especially that monasticism that had its origins in both the Cluniac and Cistercian reform movements of an earlier time.[12] This ideal, according to Sabatier, was compromised both by the less idealistic members of his own fraternity who could not live up to such ideals and by the institutional Church as a whole which saw the movement as a threat to their own power and hegemony over the vast body of the Christian faithful. The end result of this hostility and misunderstanding was the eventual bureaucratization of the Franciscan charisma until the lay movement had been transmuted into one more highly structured monastic order. For Sabatier, Francis, especially in the last years of his life, was a man betrayed and thwarted by his confrères and neutralized by the conservative tendencies of the Roman Curia. It was this central thesis of Sabatier that caused the book to be added to the list of the *Index Librorum Prohibitorum* by the Vatican — testimony, among other things, to the attractiveness of the Sabatier thesis. It was a stroke of good fortune for the popularity of Sabatier's book that it should have been written both when the public was openly sympathetic to a new look at the medieval period and at a time when a nondogmatic and more liberal picture of Christianity was very much in vogue in continental theology. If Europe was prepared to accept Harnack's notions about the essence of Christianity, it could equally accept a picture of a genuine Christian spirit full of love for life and all that is best in the Gospel, fighting against the obscurantism of the organized Church.

Today historians would be less inclined to accept the Sabatier thesis wholeheartedly (after all, Sabatier's thesis depended, at least in part, on his own notion of religion — which was a variety of liberal Protestantism). Nonetheless, it is still true that almost every interpretative effort has used the Sabatier effort as the *terminus a quo* of critical discussion.[13] When one reads the literature produced on Francis by members of the Franciscan Order today it is obvious that they write with the spirit of Sabatier haunting their discussion. This has been more true in the contemporary period when the more liberal spirit of the post Vatican II church has permitted some of the Franciscans themselves to admit the possibility that Sabatier had more to say than had been the fashion to admit. In a sense, Sabatier's life of Saint Francis is to Franciscan studies what Jacob Burckhardt's *Civilization of the Renaissance in Italy* is to studies of that period: a thesis to be reckoned with either positively or negatively, but a thesis that cannot be ignored.

The Catholic response to Sabatier's biography, though not written just as a response but as a book that was meant to stand on its own merit, was done by the Catholic convert and Danish critic, Johannes Joergensen. Written in Danish in 1907, with simultaneous translations into French and German, it was published in English in 1912.[14] It has remained one of the classic biographies of the saint and has had an unqualified success right down to the present day. Before it was published in paperback in the United States (Image Books, 1955) *Saint Francis of Assisi: A Biography* went through fifteen printings in England alone. Joergensen's biography, also respectful of the historical sources and aware of the work of Sabatier, "reads" Francis purely and simply as a Christ-intoxicated mystic who remained a faithful and joyous son of the Church despite some personal disappointments and reverses. The great emphasis of Joergensen's biography was on Francis as mystic with the culmination of his life of Christocentric mysticism being the reception of the stigmata on Mount La Verna, a chapter that Joergensen wrote by skillfully interweaving narrative detail of his own with the sources that had described this phenomenon in the thirteenth century.[15]

Joergensen's life is a good illustration of the attractive power of the Franciscan ideal in the latter part of the nineteenth century. Joergensen was born in Denmark in 1867 and as a young man had gained a name for himself as a journalist and writer. He became a Catholic in his youth and felt a tremendous attraction for Italy and its religious heritage for, as he once said to a friend, "In Italy you can travel fifty feet off the main road and find a place where once mysticism thrived and, indeed, where mysticism thrives today."[16] In 1899 he published a Danish translation of the *Fioretti* which he had done while convalescing from an illness in Assisi. In 1902 he was in Rome on another Italian visit and met the famous Franciscan historian, Father Leonard Lemmens, O.F.M., in the Vatican library. Lemmens knew of his work on Franciscan material and told him that he would become the "Catholic Sabatier." Inspired by this confidence Joergensen traveled through Umbria and Tuscany studying the places made famous by Saint Francis. These journeys resulted in his book *Pilgrimsbogen (The Book of My Pilgrimage*, 1903) a work which must be seen as a prelude to his famous biography of the saint which was to be published in Denmark in 1907. From 1915 until the end of his life he lived intermittently in Assisi and, still under the influence of his first interest in Italian mysticism, he continued his writings in the field of hagiography and spirituality. He wrote a spiritual autobiography after a long period of meditation at the Franciscan shrine at La Verna *(Geschichte eines verborgenen Lebens*, 1912) and, after a visti to Siena, he wrote a biography of the great Dominican mystic Saint Catherine of Siena (1915). It is a sign of the preeminence of Joergensen in things Franciscan that he was chosen to offer a bouquet of roses at the tomb of Dante on the occasion of the six hundredth anniversary of the poet's death (1921) in the name of all the Franciscans of the world. In 1924 Joergensen published *Breve Fra Assisi,* a collection of his occasional pieces ranging in topic from Dante to short sketches of Italian, especially Umbrian, life. He edited for a time a journal on Franciscan themes (*Frate Francesco*), served as editor for a series of books on cities of Italy, and continued to write. The most famous work of his later years was an important biography of Saint Brigid of Sweden, a two-volume work which he completed in 1941.

In the early 1920s Joergensen mèt a young Greek who had come to Assisi as a part of his pilgrimage to solve his religious struggles. This young man, Nikos Kazantzakis, was much impressed. He was later to recall in his autobiographical work *Report to Greco* how he and Johannes Joergensen walked the streets of Assisi discussing the saint and his significance as a religious teacher and as a mystical mentor.[17] This interest in the Franciscan style of life was intensified later when Kazantzakis met a living man whom he regarded as a new Saint Francis: Albert Schweitzer. Both Saint Francis and Schweitzer had been inspired into action by the imperative of the Christian Gospel, both had a love for music, a reverence for nature, and both forsook comfortable lives to give themselves to the service of others.

Out of this matrix of ideas and persons emerged Kazantzakis's fictionalized biography of the saint, *Saint Francis* (1962). Told from the perspective of the old Brother Leo, Francis's companion and former secretary, there is nothing in this book reminiscent of the sometime saccharine hagiography one finds in lives of saints, and especially lives of Saint Francis. Kazantzakis is not overly concerned with historical accuracy in his account and he explicitly admits the imaginative and nonhistorical character of the book in the introduction. The Saint Francis that emerges from the account of Kazantzakis loses any hint of the ethereal, near-docetic treatment that often burdens legends of the saint in popular writing. The Francis of Kazantzakis feels a sexual attraction for the young Clare; wrestles with the naked woman of temptation just as the great desert fathers of the Thebiad days had done; is revolted by the sight of leprosy; beats his own body ("Brother Ass") into ascetic submission. God sorely tests Francis — has him "writhing in his claws" as Kazantzakis writes — and when Francis cries out for the Resurrection at the time of the stigmatization on Mount La Verna God tells him that "crucifixion, resurrection, and paradise are one." This struggle of the human as he attempts to ascend to the Divine haunted Kazantzakis all his life, runs as a *leitmotiv* through many of his novels, and is the very theme of *Report to Greco*. It was this struggle that fascinated Kazantzakis as he studied Francis and it was for this reason that he was once able to write to his wife "Saint Francis had preached more accessible ideas, his teachings would have had no influence."[18]

Kazantzakis was not interested in the Saint Francis of the nature legend. His fascination, as his novel and his other comments clearly demonstrate, came from the willingness of Saint Francis to take a hard and unflinching look at reality at its worst and best and try to sanctify it. When Joergensen asked Kazantzakis why he loved Saint Francis so much, the Greek author at first replies because Saint Francis was able to find divinity in the smallest of creatures; Joergensen pressed him for another reason and Kazantzakis replied: "Second, I love him because by means of love and ascetic discipline his soul conquered reality — hunger, disease, cold, scorn, injustice, ugliness (what men without wings call reality) and succeeded in transubstantiating this reality into a joyous dream truer than truth itself."[19]

Later in his life when Kazantzakis met Schweitzer he thought of many parallels between the two men: both loved animals, both had a great love for music, and an intense compassion for everything that suffered. But beyond that, Kazantzakis saw in Schweitzer the same characteristic that he confessed to Joergensen many years before that he had loved in Saint Francis: "They [Francis and Schweitzer] take disease, hunger, cold, injustice, ugliness — reality at its most horrible — and transubstantiate these into a reality yet more real where the wind of spirit blows. No, not of spirit; of love."[20]

This harsh ascetical side of Saint Francis emphasized by Nikos Kazantzakis has been a source of attraction for others in our own notoriously nonascetic time. The seriousness of Saint Francis was one of the motivating factors in the religious conversion of the woman who has been called the "mystic of the death of God — Simone Weil.[21] Although she never wrote any systematic work on Saint Francis (in fact, she wrote very few systematic works on any topic — her claim to fame rests mainly on fragmentary and unfinished works) her letters and diaries, published after her death, bear abundant witness to the influence that Saint Francis had on her life and thought. When she visited Assisi in 1937 she used the *Fioretti*, the

Lives of Celano and Bonaventure, and the *Paradiso* of Dante as her guide to discover the *genius loci* of Assisi. She recalls in a letter that it was while she was visiting the little Romanesque church of Santa Maria degli Angeli (now housed inside an ugly and pretentious Baroque basilica) that she felt, for the first time in her life, the need to kneel down and pray. In the ensuing years, as she led out her tragic existence in flight from Nazi persecution in France and work with the Free French in London, her writings harken back to Francis who so inspired her own search for an understanding of the significance of poverty and abandonment. She once confided to her mentor and spiritual advisor, Father Perrin of Marseilles, that "I fell in love with Saint Francis as soon as I came to know him."[22]

What was it about Saint Francis that attracted this woman who was, in the words of one of her biographers and translators, Richard Rees, so singularly deficient in so many of the typical Franciscan virtues? In the early days of her religious development, which were coterminous with the time she had visited Assisi, Simone Weil saw Saint Francis as a living *apologia* for the credibility and the spiritual possibilities of Christianity. In a typically apodictic statement she once said to a friend that except for Saint Francis the whole of Christianity had lost any sense of the beauty of the world. It was in the life of Saint Francis that she intuited the true essence of the religious experience: the ability to synthesize within oneself an outlook on creation as a true gift from God combined with compassionate concern for neighbor based on the love of God. She summed this attitude up well in a letter that she once wrote to her spiritual director, Father Perrin: "We have to be Catholic, that is to say, not bound by so much as a thread to any created thing unless it be creation in its totality. Formerly, in the case of the saints, it was impossible for this universality to be implicit; even in their own consciousness, they were able to give the rightful place in their soul, on the one hand to the love due only to God and to all his creation, and on the other, to their obligation to all that was smaller than the universe. I think that Saint Francis and Saint John of the Cross were like this: that is why they were both of them poets."[23]

The serious and mystical side of Saint Francis is not the only facet of his life that has received the attention of modern writers. The "romantic" Saint Francis has also had a continuing influence on the modern temper. A case in point is Hermann Hesse. Hesse was intensely interested in the medieval period when he was a young man and out of this early interest came two monographs now long out of print: *Franz von Assisi* (1904) and *Boccaccio* (1950). His biographical study of the saint was mostly aesthetic in its orientation, concentrating on Francis as a poet and as an aesthetic inspirer of art, especially the art of Giotto. Hesse published his monograph on Francis the same year, 1904, that he achieved literary success with the first of his novels, *Peter Camenzind.*[24] The novel, in the familiar genre of the German *Bildungsroman*, chronicles the education and intellectual pilgrimage of an aspiring young writer who leaves the rural life of Switzerland in order to pursue his lifework. His travels take him to Assisi where he comes into contact with the simple life of the people and the memory, still very much alive, of the saint of Assisi. His later encounters with the intellectual circles of Zurich and the bohemian life of Paris leave him totally unsatisfied with his life both as a person and as an artist. In the last part of the novel he strikes up a friendship with a crippled workman named Boppi — against all of his natural inclinations. From this simple person he learns a great deal about life and the wisdom of simple people. It is with this simple man that he begins to learn about the true nature of life and he stays with Boppi until the man dies.

The whole of *Peter Camenzind* is directed to the self-understanding that Peter achieves through his contact with Boppi in the latter part of the book. Hesse suffuses the last part of the work with a spirit of Franciscan humanism as the aspiring artist learns that external success and superficial human relationships will not bring him either happiness or insight. From the example of Boppi and from the lessons of Assisis he discovers that happiness has little to do with mundane success. Happiness, Hesse insists, comes from an awareness of the guidance of providence, from the maturing influence of pain and suffering, from a tender and constant love of nature, from rootedness in the world of nature, and, finally, from a sense of the possibilities inherent in the service of others (symbolized by his care of the ailing Boppi), after the example of Saint Francis. In this early novel Saint Francis becomes the paradigmatic model for the alleviation of artistic and human alienation. Hesse, of course, was not to continue this paradigm in his later writings; under the influence of his studies of Eastern thought and his own encounters with Jungian analysis he would deepen and expand his ideas of human integration but at the very beginning of his career he was very much a part of the romantic interest in the saint and his ideals.

This emphasis on the "romantic" Saint Francis is also seen in the brilliant, if eccentric, biography of Saint Francis that was published by Gilbert Keith Chesterton in 1923. Long before he had become a

Catholic, Chesterton had shown an interest in the saint and one of his earlier publications had been a long essay on the saint published in a volume with other essays of a religious nature, including a study of the religious ideas of Leo Tolstoy.[25] With an invitation extended to him by the publishing firm of Hodder and Stoughton to contribute a volume on the saint for their "People's Library" series, Chesterton was able to return to the saint who had so obviously fascinated him in the earlier days of his journalistic career. The biography, entitled *Saint Francis of Assisi*, was typical of Chesterton's other biographical efforts: little biographical information was provided, that which did appear was often shaky with respect to dates and/or places, and there was little in the way of continuous biographical narrative. This cavalier attitude towards the biographical style was not atypical in Chesterton; nonetheless, Dudley Barker has written, "Chesterton recovered in this book his special clarity of portraiture which depended scarcely at all upon facts (or even, sometimes, upon accuracy) but upon a simple viewpoint and the ability to describe a complex characteristic in a few incisive phrases."[26] Saint Francis, according to Chesterton, was preeminently a man of thanksgiving who had a profound awareness of the goodness of the world as it came from the creative hand of God who pronounced it good in the very act of making it. For Chesterton, Francis was able to show men how to appreciate the beauty and the sacramentality of the created world without falling into the pagan error of ever divinizing the cosmos. Above all, Francis blended his instinct for poetry into the very fabric of his existence so that his view of the world was at the same time realistic (he understood the world as real and good) and wonder-filled. Francis, like Thomas Aquinas, had a great love of God's creation that never trailed off into sterile abstractions about "mankind" or "nature" (he never used either word). Francis was interested in the particularities of creation. "A philanthropist," Chesterton wrote, "may be said to love anthropoids, but as Saint Francis did not love humanity but men, so he did not love Christianity, but Christ."[27]

Besides the major biographies of Sabatier and Joergensen and the lesser biographical efforts of men such as Chesterton that we have already had occasion to mention, this century has seen a great stream of other biographies, too extensive even to mention: Raphael Brown's Franciscan bibliography mentions over twenty-five books and his list does not pretend to be a definitive one.[28] Mention must be made of some of the more significant of these works.

The English Capuchin, Father Cuthbert of Brighton, published a

Life of Saint Francis (London, 1912) that enjoyed a great popularity in the earlier part of this century while the great Anglican scholar John Moorman (now Anglican bishop of Ripon) published a short life of the saint in 1963 and a lengthy history of the Franciscan Order later, these works being the culmination of many years of active research into Franciscan lore that date back to 1940. Omer Englebert's *Vie de Saint Françis* (Paris, 1947) was translated into English and then updated by the American Franciscanist, Ignatius Brady, O.F.M. This *Life of Saint Francis* (Chicago, 1965) is conventional enough as a biography but Brady's updating plus the inclusion of Raphael Brown's extensive bibliography, and the numerous important historical appendices makes this biography an indispensable tool for further study and research. In Italy, there have been any number of biographies of the saint both by lay scholars (Bargellini and Papini) and Franciscans (Gemelli and Facchinetti) but the most important of these biographies is the five-volume *Nova Vita di San Francisco* (Assisi, 1959) by Arnoldo Fortini. Fortini, once the mayor of Assisi, has an unparalleled knowledge of early archival sources relating to the period of Saint Francis in his own town in the whole area of Umbria. Many scholars have been critical of Fortini's interpretations and analyses but his biography is an indispensable research tool because of the copious original sources that he has published on the saint and his milieu.

In a more contemporary vein, Saint Francis has been the center of some attraction for those who are interested in his attitude toward the natural world of creation, as a possible clue to our attitudes toward nature and the whole question of ecology. The most significant essay dealing with this question is Lynn White's "The Historical Roots of our Ecological Crisis."[29] This essay argues that Francis was the greatest religious revolutionary that the Western world produced precisely because he "tried to substitute the idea of the equality of all creatures, including man, for the idea of man's limitless rule of creation." White admits that his notion of the spiritual autonomy of all parts of nature was an important insight and, for that reason alone, has proposed Saint Francis as "the patron saint of ecologists."

Saint Francis, of course, has always been identified in the popular mind with the creatures of the world and this identification has not always been totally free of a cloying sentimentality. Rene Dubos, for example, thinks that the pragmatic and sensible Saint Benedict of Nursia would be a better patron of ecology than White's Saint Francis on the grounds that Francis was too much of a mystic and visionary.[30] Hence, any study of the saint that puts his views on nature into some sort of perspective is welcome. On a theoretical level Chesterton's work was a step in the right direction even though it was eccentric but one is also grateful for a recent historical study: Edward Armstrong's *Saint Francis: Nature Mystic* (Berkeley, 1973). Armstrong's book is a fascinating, if not totally convincing, example of solid cross-disciplinary study. Armstrong is a naturalist by profession who, besides his technical studies in various aspects of ornithology, has interested himself in historical studies of problems that center around the areas germane to the naturalist. His work on Saint Francis not only tries to shed light on the nature stories as they are told in the early biographies, but attempts to follow their genesis and elaboration by drawing on analogous sources in Celtic hagiography and possible Eastern sources. Franciscan scholars may cavil at some of the less secure leaps that Armstrong attempts, but his overall study is indicative of the continuing fascination that Saint Francis holds over persons of the most disparate interests. It is Armstrong's conclusion that Saint Francis is important in the development of Western culture for reasons that go well beyond his exemplary life as a Christian since "he was not only a naturalist but a man whose loving sympathy for all aspects of creation invigorated his insight, pioneering the way for the poets, artists, and scientists."[31]

The centrality of Saint Francis in the development of the Western cultural tradition has been vigorously argued in the writings of the Viennese intellectual historian Friedrich Heer. Heer has insisted that, in a very real sense, Francis was a living critic to the many powerful forces struggling to emerge as the leading shaper of the future in the turmoil of the thirteenth century — forces, were any of them to succeed, that would determine the future of our Western civilization. Saint Francis of Assisi stood as a symbolic message to all of these eddying currents of the medieval world: "To the Cathars the message ran: 'God is not only pure spirit' but also wholly man, vulnerable, helpless, bleeding flesh, the blood of brother men, too precious to be shed in warfare of any kind; To Byzantium and the Eastern Church it said: Even in His Transfiguration, Christ still appears to us poor men in His crucified body; To Rome, the church which claimed to rule the emperors and kings of the world, it said: Christ came to earth to be servants of His own. The war mad Italian towns, standing for embattled Christendom as a whole, were reminded that Christians were called to be peacemakers."[32]

The significance both of Saint Francis and the whole Franciscan movement is still subject to the scrutiny of professional historians of the Western cultural tradition. Only in more recent days have historians began to comprehend fully the immense ramifications — social, political, cultural, and philosophical — of the Spiritual Franciscans. The immense impact of the Franciscan school of philosophy (encompassing such figures as Bonaventure, Scotus, and William of Ockham) on later philosophical thought and theological revisionism (especially in the Reform movements) is receiving much critical attention. Recent studies on the later medieval period, a time which prepared the emergence of the Reformation and, by extension, the modern world, saw the Franciscans as being in the forefront; indeed, as Heiko Oberman has observed about the late medieval period: "It is not surprising that the Franciscans proved to be in tune with the *Zeitgeist;* so much so that for two centuries late medieval spirituality, piety, and theology outside the university halls can be said to have been dominated by them."[33]

While this important scholarly work goes on apace, others, by no means professional historians or theologians, have continued to be fascinated by the figure of the Poor Man of Assisi. Joan Erikson, wife of the noted psychoanalyst Erik Erikson,[34] has written a lovely impressionistic study of the saint entitled *Saint Francis and His Four Ladies* (New York, 1970) which is an interpretation of the saint's life from the perspective of the four women, real and symbolic, who most influenced his life: Lady Pica, his mother; Lady Poverty; Saint Clare of Assisi; and Mary, the Virgin Queen of Heaven. The most interesting and provocative chapter in this short book is the one on Lady Pica, the mother of the saint. Lady Pica had originally come from Provence and Joan Erikson believes that it was from her and her provençal background that Francis inherited his taste for the *chanson* and its courtly tradition to a degree that he later was also known as the *jongleur de Dieu*. This tradition also paid a great deal of attention to the refinements of "courtesy" in its acting out of the courtly love tradition. Francis utilized this notion of "courtesy" though in a less mundane way; in fact, Francis can be said to have elaborated a theology of courtesy. Courtesy, Francis insisted, was an attribute of God; it was a sister to charity and drove out hatred while nurturing love. Erikson insists that it was the Lady Pica who first instructed Francis in the centrality of this concept and that it was for her that "one is inclined to trace in Saint Francis the courteous relationships with the other ladies who were part of his life, and indeed his courtesy to all men and to all things . . ."[35]

After nearly one hundred years of serious historical scholarship, scholarship that continues unabated at a high level of quality to our own day, a totally satisfactory biography of the saint has yet to appear which takes into account not only the complex world of the twelfth and thirteenth centuries, but the far-reaching impact Francis had on subsequent culture. The groundwork has been done but the biographer has yet to come forward, a biographer free from *parti pris* considerations and with the fruits of scholarship at his disposal.

Francis Holland Smith has recently published a new biography of the saint, *Francis of Assisi* (New York, 1972). This biography does not betray high-level competence with the historical sources nor does it show a consistent interpretation of Francis or his long-ranging significance. Yet there is merit in this biography, admittedly written by a nonspecialist, in that Smith attempts to come to grips with the figure of Saint Francis in terms that are free from sectarian considerations and from the vantage point of the phenomenology of religion. In the course of his study Smith attempts to show that the desire of Francis to become like Christ should be seen in the light of the category of "christification" once described by C. G. Jung; the culmination of this attempt at "christification" occurred at La Verna with the stigmata when Francis then took on the characteristics of the Jungian "cosmic man." Unfortunately, Smith does not maintain the focus of this Jungian perspective throughout the biography and, as a result of other categorizations, the overall portrait of the saint becomes muddied. The great merit of Smith's biography is his attempt, failure though it is, to lift the life of Francis out of the conventional hagiographical framework. His own attempt at a new framework does give a clue as to one interpretative approach that would be possible to pursue in any future biography. It might be quite possible to see Francis in terms of the categories worked out by such scholars of the phenomenology of religion as Eliade, Van der Leeuw, and others. It might be quite legitimate to study Saint Francis not as just a medieval Catholic saint but in the far broader category of shaman or prophet. Such an approach would both illuminate the character of the man and demonstrate his significance on a plane that would transcend both the Christian and the Western category in which he is often placed. Francis, in my opinion, is a religious figure of world significance and should be seen in that light. Hence, I welcome discussions such as Winston King's comparison of Saint Francis and the nineteenth century Hindu mystic Ramakrisna as complementary examples of devotional mysticism.[36] Such discussions, done with methodological rigor, do not denigrate a particular tradition nor are they attempts at a Pollyannaish ecumenism; they are, rather, testimony to the universal nature of the religious experience.

Our century, for all its advance in Franciscan historiography and interpretation, has yet to replicate the equivalent of Sabatier's pioneering biography. There has not been a book in our time that sets the stage for further discussion of the significance of Francis, and that discussion needs a new basis today. It is obvious that the religious ideals of Saint Francis are still a source of inspiration for some of the most attractive religious activists of our day — *vide* Dorothy Day of the Catholic Worker Movement and Mother Teresa of Calcutta. Yet the relevance of Saint Francis goes in many directions. There are clues in his life and message that speak to many of the concerns of contemporary people; issues such as peace and brotherhood; respect for the created universe and the amelioration of human suffering; a thirst for beauty and an exaltation of the sense of poetry obtainable in human life. Saint Francis, then, remains as a source for wonder and as a paradox for meditation; he simultaneously symbolized in his own age all that was best in the medieval era while serving as a critique that was incipiently dangerous about that age. In the polyfaceted personality of this attractive man there is still much to ponder, both for instruction and for inspiration.

It must also be remembered that the Franciscan Order still lives inside the Roman Catholic Church. The three great branches of the male religious order (the Friars Minor, the Conventuals, and the Capuchins) are joined by the followers of the Third Order Regular and the Poor Clares among the female religious. Enumerable small diocesan and/or regional congregations of sisters and friars follow some modified version of the Franciscan Rule. It is important to keep that in mind since many of the writings that have been studied in the course of this book have only a literary or cultural interest for the majority while for the few those writings are literally a rule of life and a guide for conduct.

The Franciscan Orders, both male and female, are extremely large in the Roman Catholic Church and they continue to witness to the vitality of the Franciscan ideal as it is exemplified in community life. What is not as well known and appreciated is that the Franciscan rule of life has also been adopted by Anglicans and that groups of religious, both male and female, exist in the Anglican Communion. Anglican religious orders sprang into existence as a consequence of the romanizing tendencies of the Oxford Movement in the last century. There was an Anglican community of women in 1845 and one for men in 1866. These religious orders received their inspiration and the initial impetus for their foundation from a renewed interest in the early Church sources, from a study of early monasticism, from the Victorian desire to rediscover the medieval world, and from a spirit of imitating the religious fashions of continental Christianity (i.e., Catholicism). Curiously enough, this revival of the religious life, coming from the Oxford Movement did not produce a Franciscan brotherhood; the Anglican Franciscans, first founded in 1892, grew from a different inspiration and a different source than the other Anglican religious Orders; Anglican Franciscanism ". . . was inspired by another strand in the Church of the last century in England — a strong evangelical and social conscience. Put very briefly, the first Franciscan brotherhood began in 1892 in the slums of London and was called the Society of Divine Compassion."[37]

This first foundation, dedicated to social work, good deeds, preaching and prayer, was followed by the founding of other groups of religious using the inspiration of the Franciscan ideal of life: the Brotherhood of the Love of Christ, the Community of Saint Francis, the Brotherhood of Saint Francis of Assisi. For all intents and purposes, these groups were later merged into what is now called the Society of Saint Francis. The Society of Saint Francis adopted to its own needs the primitive rule of Saint Francis and has specialized in working with the needy and destitute. There are Anglican Franciscan houses in England, the United States, Australia, New Guinea, and the Solomon Islands. The Anglican Franciscans are primarily a lay community and hold no property of their own. In order to deepen their contemplative life, the brothers are experimenting with hermitages and, in a nice ecumenical touch, are trying to establish these retreats so much beloved by the early Franciscans, in conjunction with French Capuchin Franciscans of the Roman Catholic Church.

One of the more interesting of the Anglican Franciscan groups of religious was the Society of the Atonement founded in New York by the Reverend Paul Watson in 1898. His goal was to found an Anglican religious order that would be modelled on the Roman Catholic American Order of the Paulists founded some years earlier by Isaac Hecker. Watson's Society of the Atonement had a female branch under the aegis of Mother Lurana Mary White (1870-1935). Because of the indifference and, at times, overt hostility of the Anglican Church in America, Father Paul, as he came to be known, eventually led his group, Mother Lurana, and her group into the Roman Catholic Church. They were received into the Church of Rome in 1909 and were later established as a Roman Catholic religious order. The Catholic Society of the Atonement has thrived and has specialized in an apostolate of ecumenical concern both by prayer and work. The group still follows the Franciscan rule of life.

Finally, it should be noted that Saint Francis has been a great symbol for those who have been interested in the ecumenical movement, especially as it relates to the unity of all Christians. The Franciscan spirit has been most helpful here. Even today one finds in Assisi groups of devout Protestants and Orthodox who share an enthusiasm for the beautiful mystical spirit of Saint Francis. The present writer remembers with pleasure staying at a hostel in Assisi while doing some research into the life of the saint and sharing accommodations with some Swiss Evangelicals who had come with their pastor for a week of prayer and meditation.

In the earlier part of this century it was Friedrich Heiler who proposed the ideal of Saint Francis as a bridge between Protestants and Catholics with the greatest clarity and theological precision. Heiler, who had devoted his life to bridging the religious experience of disparate believers, had been a student of the great phenomenologist of religion, Rudolph Otto. In Heiler's own ground-breaking study of the phenomenology of prayer (*Das Gebet,* published in 1918) he first began to study Saint Francis because he felt that Francis was a veritable paragon of prayer and the life of prayer. In Heiler's later work on the character of the Roman Catholic Church (*Der Katholizimus,* published in 1923) Saint Francis, along with Aquinas, Augustine, and a few others becomes for Heiler a prototypal figure of the essence of Catholicism. Yet, this essentially Catholic saint was a person who transcended his own confessional background, and as far as Heiler was concerned, Francis became the Christian who most inspired a hope that the bridge between Catholic and Reform Christianity was a possibility.

Heiler gave clearest expression to this idea of the ecumenical stature of Saint Francis in a lecture that he delivered in 1926 at Oxford and at Cambridge Universities. Heiler began by reminding his audience that Saint Francis exercised a great influence over noble Protestant minds (e.g., Nathan Söderbloom, Ernest Renan, Paul Sabatier, among others) in the modern period. Heiler does not accept the notion, however, that Saint Francis was an undogmatic liberal Christian (*pace* Sabatier) or a quasi-pantheist in the mold of Goethe or Rabindrinath Tagore. For Heiler, the active mysticism of Saint Francis was based on his grasp of the two central mysteries of Christianity, the Incarnation and the Atonement. Heiler also asserted that Saint Francis was a devoted and orthodox son of the Roman Catholic Church all his life. This devotion to the Church meant that Saint Francis was also a convinced sacramentalist; Heiler asserts that anyone who knew anything at all about the life of the saint would be convinced of his devotion both to the sacrament of Penance and the Holy Eucharist. Heiler spent a fair amount of time in his lecture to establish his point about the Catholicity of the saint precisely because he recognized that there were elements in the life of this Catholic saint so compelling to the Protestant mind that they would be able to see their own concerns writ large in the life of a quintessential Roman Catholic. What are these elements? In the first place, the simple desire of Saint Francis, reiterated all of his life and in all of his writings, that everyone should follow the evangelical life, i.e., the desire of the saint that all be evangelical Christians. Secondly, Saint Francis had an enormous respect for the Bible, and insisted that the written Word of God be afforded the same respect as the Holy Eucharist. Finally, Heiler notes, if Saint Francis never preached the Lutheran idea of the assurance of grace, he certainly lived it. It is no coincidence, Heiler notes, that Luther taught that the proof of possession of the Holy Spirit was joy and that Paul Sabatier wrote that the characteristic of Franciscan spirituality was the notion of *laetitia* (joy or happiness) — that joy, Heiler writes, "which irradiates the whole life of Saint Francis and his disciples, has according to his own avowal its roots in the assurance of grace which is guaranteed in God's promises."

Heiler concluded his lecture with an invitation to the Reformed Church to look to Saint Francis as a bridge figure to the Catholics; he concluded that the Catholics, in turn, had much to learn from Saint Francis. Heiler's words seem almost prophetic today in the Christian world after Pope John, but they also contain essentially Franciscan truths not only for Catholics but for all persons of good will:

But not only the non-Roman but likewise the Roman Christians have to learn from Saint Francis. They must learn to embrace all separated brethren with the love of the Poverello. It is this Franciscan love in which so many members of the present-day Roman Church are lacking, and we miss it especially in some documents of the Roman hierarchy. The unity of the Roman and the non-Roman Churches cannot be realised until the occupant of the *cathedra Petri* becomes similar to that *minister generalis* whose portrait Saint Francis has shown to us. Once towards the end of his life when one of the brethren asked the saint to name a man within the brotherhood upon whom his spirit reposed and who would be worthy to become a *minister generalis,* Saint Francis answered: "I do not see anyone who would be able to lead such a great and widespread flock: but I will try to give you a description of him." And Saint Francis drew in a wonderful way the portrait of the *minister generalis* who would be a good shepherd and a real Vicar of Christ. One of his sayings is: "Ut protervos in mansuetudinem flectat, seipsum prosternat, et aliquid sui iuris relaxet, ut animum lucrifaciat." "In order to humble the proud, he shall humiliate *himself* and give up something of his claims in order to win their souls."[38]

Notes and References

Chapter One

1. John Moorman, *The Sources For The Life of Saint Francis of Assisi* (Manchester, England 1940), p. 16 (hereafter cited as *Sources*). Moorman has a discussion on the various attempts to classify Saint Francis's writings.

2. Cited in Marion A. Habig, ed., *Saint Francis of Assisi: English Omnibus of the Sources for the Life of Saint Francis* (Chicago, 1973), p. 68 (hereafter cited as *Omnibus*). The most comprehensive single volume of its kind. Where I wish my own translation, I will cite from Lawrence S. Cunningham, ed., *Brother Francis: Writings by and about Saint Francis of Assisi* (New York, 1972). The Latin writings of the saint can be found in *Opuscula Sancti Patris Francisci Assisiensis* (Quaracchi, 1904 - 1949).

3. For the attempts to reconstruct this primitive rule, cf. John Moorman, *Sources*, pp. 38 - 54; Armando Quaglia, *Origine e sviluppo della regola francescana* (Napoli, 1947); Lothar Hardick, "The Rule in its Development and Early Observance," in *The Marrow of the Gospel*, edited by Ignatius Brady (Chicago, 1958), p. 18 ff. The methodology of this reconstruction has been to eliminate all of the scriptural citations from the *Rule of 1221* (which had been added by Caesar of Speyer) and all of the sections that seem to be provable later additions based on developments within the order during the decade 1210 - 1220. With all that, the final text of the lost primitive rule still must remain conjectural.

4. John Moorman, *A History of the Franciscan Order* (Oxford, 1968), p. 53 - 54.

5. Cf. the *Vita Prima* of Thomas of Celano in *Omnibus*, p. 412 - 13.

6. The complete text is in *Omnibus*, pp. 31 - 53.

7. The complete text is found in *Omnibus*, pp. 57 - 64.

8. See prologue to the *Speculum Perfectionis* in *Omnibus*, p. 1125.

9. Introduction to Paul Sabatier, *Vie de Saint François D'Assise* (Paris, 1894); a complete translation of that introduction may be found in *Brother Francis*, p. 26. On the thesis of Sabatier, cf. also Friedrich Heer, *The Intellectual History of Europe*, Vol. I. (Garden City, 1968), p. 179. It is a testimony to the persuasive power of Sabatier's thesis that, two generations after, Lothar Hardick in his study of the early *Rule* should feel constrained

to write that his study is an answer to positions advanced by Paul Sabatier: "All too much of current writing on Saint Francis is permeated with the thesis of Sabatier, that the Rule was somehow forced upon the saint and is at least a compromise in which he had to sacrifice what was dearest to him. This has become almost a dogma in many biographies and modern studies of the Poverello"; introduction to *art. cit.*, p. 3.

10. *Omnibus*, p. 55 - 6.

11. John Moorman, *A History*, p. 58.

12. Heer, *Intellectual History of Europe* I, p. 182.

13. The writings of Clare are found in Ignatius Brady, ed., *The Legends and Writings of Saint Clare of Assisi* (Saint Bonaventure, New York, 1953).

14. *Omnibus*, p. 76.

15. Thomas of Celano, *Vita Prima*. Cap. 9. in *Omnibus*, p. 246.

16. Vittorio Facchinetti, *Gli scritti di San Francesco D'Assisi* (Milan, 1967), p. 86 - 7.

17. *Omnibus*, p. 72.

18. Jacques Cambell. "Les Écrits de Saint François devant la critique," *Franziskanische Studien* XXXVI (1954), p. 213.

19. *Omnibus*, p. 73.

20. Thomas Merton, "Franciscan Eremitism," in *Contemplation in a World of Action* (Garden City, 1971), p. 263 ff.

21. Cajetan Esser, *The Origins of the Franciscan Order* (Chicago, 1970), p. 162.

22. *Legend of the Three Companions*, cap. 14. *Omnibus*, p. 540.

23. Cambell, "Les Écrits," pp. 207 - 8.

24. Admonition #8. *Omnibus*, p. 82.

25. Esser, *Origins*, p. 269, footnote 215.

26. John Moorman, *A History*, p. 77. The definitive study of this document is: Cajetan Esser, *Das Testament des Heiligen Francis von Assisi* (Munster, 1949); cf. also Auspicius Van Corstanje, *The Covenant With God's Poor: An Essay on the Biblical Interpretation of the Testament of Saint Francis of Assisi* (Chicago, 1966).

27. I use my translation in this section: *Brother Francis*, p. 50; the text is also found in *Omnibus*, p. 67 ff.

28. *Ibid*, pp. 52 - 3. On the whole question of poverty in early Franciscanism, cf. M. D. Lambert, *Franciscan Poverty* (London, 1961).

29. *Brother Francis*, p. 110.

30. J. Cambell, "Les Écrits", p. 250.

31. *Omnibus*, p. 76.

32. The text of the letters of Francis is in *Omnibus*, p. 92 ff.; the letter to Brother Leo is on p. 118. The entire letter reads:

Brother Leo, send peace and greetings to your Brother Francis. As a mother to her child, I speak to you, my son. In this one word, in this one piece of advice, I want to sum up all that we said on our journey, and, in case hereafter you still find it necessary to come to me for advice, I want to say this to you: In whatever way you think you will best please our Lord God and follow in his footsteps and in poverty, take that way with the Lord God's blessing and my obedience. And if you find it necessary for your peace of soul or your own consolation and you want to come to me, Leo, then come.

33. John Moorman, *Sources*, p. 22.
34. Text in *Omnibus*, p. 93 ff.
35. Thus it is placed with the *Rule For Hermitages* and not with the letters in the Quaracchi edition of 1904.
36. Text in *Omnibus*, p. 100 ff.
37. This letter is not accepted as authentic by all writers; cf. Jacques Cambell, "Les Écrits," p. 254 ff. The text is found in *Omnibus*, p. 115 ff.
38. Text in *Omnibus*, p. 102 ff.
39. The impact of early Franciscanism on the development of the Roman liturgy has been immense; the fundamental study of this question is: Stephen Van Dijk and J. H. Walker, *The Origins of the Modern Roman Liturgy: The Liturgy of the Roman Court & the Franciscan Order in the Thirteenth Century* (Westminister, Md., 1960).
40. Text in *Omnibus*, p. 112 ff.
41. Text in *Omnibus*, p. 109 ff.
42. Wadding's work is: *Beati Patris Francisci Assisiantis Opuscula* (Rome, 1623); for a profile of the man, see Beningnus Millet, "Wadding, Luke," *New Catholic Encyclopedia* XIV (New York, 1968), pp. 761 - 62.
43. Boehmer's *Analekten zur Geschichte des Franciscus von Assisi* (1904) omits it while the Quaracchi Father's edition of the *Opuscula* (1904) includes it as an authentic letter.
44. Facchinetti, *Gli scritti*, p. 198.
45. *Ibid.*, p. 200.
46. This study is described in *Omnibus*, pp. 163 - 64.
47. *Omnibus*, p. 164, quoting the original research.
48. This incident can be found in my translation: *Brother Francis*, pp. 126 - 27.
49. Facchinetti, *Gli scritti*, p. 203.
50. Cambell, "Les Écrits," p. 264.
51. Lother Hardick, *art. cit.* pp. 13 - 14.
52. Cap. 68; in *Omnibus*, p. 1197.
53. The literature on Franciscan spirituality and mysticism is immense and continues to grow; there are exhaustive bibliographies on the subject. I have been most helped by the succinct, yet authoritative, account s.v. "Freres Mineurs": I *Saint Francois D'Assise* and III *Spiritualite Franciscaine: 1226 - 1517* in *Dictionnaire de Spiritualité, Ascetique, et Mystique* V (Paris, 1964), col. 1268 ff.

Chapter Two

1. *Vita Secunda*, cap. XX in *Omnibus*, p. 406. The same story is repeated in the *Considerations of the Stigmata* which is appended to the *Fioretti;* cf.

The Little Flowers of Saint Francis, ed. Serge Hughes (New York, 1964), p. 157.

2. *Brother Francis*, pp. 191 - 92.

3. *Vita Secunda*, cap. CLXXXIX in *Omnibus*, p. 513.

4. *Brother Francis*, pp. 194 - 95.

5. *Vita Secunda*, cap. CXCVIII in *Omnibus*, p. 521.

6. *Brother Francis*, p. 196.

7. C. H. Bagley, "Litany of Loreto," *Catholic Encyclopedia*, VIII, pp. 790 - 91.

8. Discussed in *Omnibus*, pp. 137 - 39.

9. There is a discussion and a complete version of this Office in *Omnibus*, pp. 140 - 55.

10. Cajetan Esser, "*Melius Catholice Observemus:* An Explanation of the Rule of the Order in the Light of the Writings and Other Words of Saint Francis," in *The Marrow of the Gospel*, ed. Ignatius Brady (Chicago, 1958), p. 132.

11. The Rule of the "Third Order" can be found in *Omnibus*, pp. 168 - 75.

12. On this dispute, see Omer Englebert, *Saint Francis of Assisi*. (Chicago, 1972), appendix VIII, p. 445 ff.

13. Vittore Branca, "Il Cantico di Frate Sole," *Archivium Franciscanum Historicum* XLI (1949), pp. 1 - 87, has an excellent discussion of the poem; also see the excellent survey by Ignazio Baldelli, "Il Cantico di Frate Sole," in *San Francesco nella ricerca storica degli ultimi ottanta anni* (Todi, 1971), pp. 77 - 94; also useful for an extended discussion of the sources: G. Getto, "Francesco D'Assisi e Il Cantico di Frate Sole," in *Letteratura Religiosa Dal Due al Novencento* (Firenze, 1967), p. 30 ff.

14. Englebert, p. 320.

15. *Brother Francis*, p. 67.

16. Two outstanding works of the last century should be noted: for art: H. Thode, *Franz von Assisi und die Anfänge der Kunst der Renaissance in Italien* (Berlin, 1885); for *belles lettres:* Antoine Ozanam, *Les Poetes Franciscains en Italie au Triezeme Siècle* (Paris, 1852).

17. Getto, *op. cit.*, p. 39.

18. Lynn White, Jr., "The Historical Roots of Our Ecological Crisis," *Science* (March 10, 1967), p. 1207. I have reproduced this important essay in *Brother Francis*.

19. Quoted from *Brother Francis*, p. 58. The original biography is: Gilbert Keith Chesterton, *Saint Francis of Assisi* (London, 1932).

20. Edward A. Armstrong, *Saint Francis: Nature Mystic* (Berkeley, 1973), pp. 218 - 43.

21. Facchinetti, *Gli Scritti*, pp. 168 - 69.

22. *Brother Francis*, pp. 67 - 68.

23. *Omnibus*, p. 643.

24. *Ibid.*, p. 920.

25. *Ibid.*, p. 467.

26. Getto, *op. cit.*, p. 13 ff.; cf. also P. Raja, "San Francesco e gli spirit cavallereschi," *Nuova Antologia* (1926), p. 387 ff.

27. *Vita Aegedii* quoted in Getto, p. 14.

28. *Omnibus*, pp. 896 - 97.

29. Edward Hutton, "Some Franciscan Poetry," *Dublin Review* (1928), p. 138; quoted in Moorman, *A History*, p. 267.

30. *Speculum Perfectionis*, cap. C. *Omnibus*, p. 1236.

31. F. J. E. Raby, "The Franciscan Poets," *A History of Christian Latin Poetry* (Oxford, 1927), pp. 415 - 57, is a fine survey and the basis of much of the information in this section (hereafter cited as Raby).

32. Although most sources will list Jacopone as the author of the *Stabat Mater* that view has not gone unchallenged in recent research on Jacopone. Rosanna Bettarini's *Jacopone e il Laudario Urbinate* (Florence, 1969) establishes exacting criteria for the identification of Jacopone's Italian poetry. Such criteria and a comparison with his Italian laud "Donna de Paradiso" do not lend support to the theory that Jacopone wrote the *Stabat Mater*. I am grateful to George Peck for pointing this out to me after I had confidently called Jacopone the author of the *Stabat Mater* in a review of Mancini's new edition of the Lauds (*Cross Currents* XXIV, pp. 519 - 21). Mr. Peck is the author of a new volume of Jacopone criticism *(The Fool of God)* forthcoming from the University of Alabama Press; I have not had the chance to see that volume.

33. Raja, *art. cit.*, and Raby, p. 430 ff.

34. For a sampling of these lauds, see *Laude Dugentesche*, ed. Giorgio Varanini (Padova, 1972).

35. Arnoldo Fortini, *La lauda in Assisi e le origini del teatro italiano* (Assisi, 1961).

36. The books on this tradition are numerous; I have benefitted from the following: Arturo Pompeati, *Storia della Letteratura Italiana* I (Torino, 1965); *Poeti del Duecento*, ed. Gianfranco Contini (Milano, n.d.); E. Pasquini and A. Quaglio, *Il Duecento dalle origini a Dante* (Bari, 1970).

37. Various essays on this intriguing movement can be consulted in *Il movimento dei disciplinati nel VII centenario del suo inizio* (Perugia, 1962).

38. Pompeati, *op. cit.*, p. 248.

39. Contini, *op. cit.*, pp. 12 - 13.

40. Moorman, *A History*, p. 272.

41. Cited in Pompeati, *op. cit.*, p. 267.

42. *Ibid.*, p. 269. The complete poems of Giacomino were published by E. I. May (Firenze, 1930); cf. also A. Barana, *La Gerusalemme celeste e la Babilonia infernale* (Verona, 1921).

43. Raby, *op. cit.*, p. 426.

44. On the nightingale in Franciscan legend, see Armstrong, *op. cit.*, p. 68 ff.

45. All citations of Jacopone's lauds and their numbering is from *Laude*, ed. Franco Mancini (Roma, 1974) (hereafter cited as *Laude*).

46. *Inferno*, canto III.

47. Angelo Monteverdi, "Jacopone Poeta," in *Jacopone e il suo tempo* (Todi, 1959), pp. 40 - 41.

48. *Laudi Trattato e Detti,* ed. Franca Ageno (Firenze, 1953).

49. Cf. footnote #45.

50. Monteverdi, *art. cit.,* p. 43.

51. On Jacopone and Franciscan mysticism, see Arsenio Frugoni, "Jacopone Francescano," in *Jacopone e il suo tempo* (Todi, 1959), pp. 75 - 102.

52. *Ibid.,* p. 85.

53. Evelyn Underhill, *Jacopone da Todi* (London, 1919).

54. Ferdinando Bologna, *La pittura italiana delle origini* (Erfurt, 1961) and Mario Salmi, "Cimabue e Jacopone," in *Jacopone e il suo tempo* (Todi, 1959), pp. 57 - 72. On this problem and other areas of current research on Jacopone, see Silvestro Nessi. "Jacopone da Todi al vaglio della critica moderna," *Miscellanea Francescana* LXIV (July - Dec., 1964) pp. 404 - 32.

55. Salmi *art. cit.* p. 71.

56. Francesco De Sanctis, *History of Italian Literature I,* translated from the Italian by Joan Redfern (New York, 1931), p. 36.

Chapter Three

1. *Sacrum Commercium S. Francisci cum Domina Paupertate,* ed. Patres Collegii S. Bonaventurae (Quaracchi, 1929); English translation: *Francis and His Lady Poverty,* ed. Placid Hermann, in *Omnibus,* pp. 1331 - 96. All quotations are from this translation.

2. *Omnibus,* p. 1535.

3. "Ubertin de Casale" in *Dictionnaire de Theologie Catholique* XV (Paris, 1950), col. 2031 - 34.

4. *Omnibus,* p. 1563.

5. On the theme of mystic marriages in art during this period, see Millard Meiss, *Painting in Siena and Florence After the Black Death* (New Haven, 1952), pp. 109 - 11.

6. Thomas of Celano, *Vita Prima S. Francisci* in *Analecta Franciscana* X (Quaracchi, 1941), pp. 2 - 115 (hereafter cited as *Analecta X);* English translation: *Omnibus,* pp. 225 - 356.

7. The relationship of Francis and Hugolin is treated by Kurt Selge, "Franz von Assisi und Ugolino von Ostia," in *San Francesco nella ricerca storica degli ultimi ottanta anni* (Todi, 1971), pp. 159 - 223.

8. John Moorman, *A History,* p. 280.

9. *Ibid.*

10. *Omnibus,* p. 201 - 2.

11. Bartholomew of Pisa, *De Conformitate Vitae B. Francisci ad Vitam Domini Jesu. Analecta Francescana* IV (Quaracchi, 1907 - 11).

12. *Omnibus,* p. 298 - 99.

13. *Ibid.,* p. 343.

14. Text in *Analecta X*, pp. 118 - 26.

15. *Analecta X*, pp. 333 - 74.

16. *Ibid.*, pp. 405 - 91.

17. *Ibid.* A collection of minor liturgical texts on the subject of Saint Francis begins on p. 389.

18. Latin text in *Analecta X*, pp. 127 - 268; in English: *Omnibus*, pp. 357 - 544.

19. *Analecta X*, pp. 269 - 330.

20. English text in *Omnibus*, pp. 853 - 955.

21. *Scripta Leonis, Ruffini, et Angeli Sociorum S. Francisci*, ed. Rosalind Brooke (Oxford: Clarendon Press, 1970). In *Omnibus*, pp. 957 - 1101.

22. Moorman, *Sources*, p. 99.

23. Brooke, *Scripta*, pp. 24 - 25.

24. *Omnibus*, pp. 1103 - 1265.

25. *Ibid.*, p. 1049.

26. *Ibid.*, p. 1086.

27. John Moorman, *A History*, p. 287.

28. Latin text in *Analecta X*, pp. 555 - 652; in English: *Omnibus*, pp. 627 - 788.

29. *Analecta X*, pp. 653 - 788; *Omnibus*, pp. 789 - 834.

30. Alistair Smart, *The Assisi Problem and the Art of Giotto* (Oxford: Clarendon Press, 1971).

31. B. Marinangeli, "Le Serie de affreschi giotteschi rappresentanti la vita de S. Francesco," *Miscellanea Francescana* XII (1911), p. 97 ff. The titles are reproduced in Smart, pp. 263 - 93.

32. Smart, p. 19.

33. *Ibid.*, p. 260. On other studies of this cycle, see especially Millard Meiss, *Giotto and Assisi* (New York, 1960) and Millard Meiss and Lionetto Tintori, *The Painting of the Life of Saint Francis of Assisi* (New York, 1962).

34. Silvestro Nessi, "La vita di San Francesco dipinta da Benozzo Gozzoli," *Miscellanea Francescana* LXI (1961), pp. 467 - 92. On the whole question of Franciscan iconography, George Kaftal, *Saint Francis in Italian Painting* (London, 1950) and *idem, The Iconography of the Saints in Tuscan Painting* (Florence, 1952) s.v. Saint Francis of Assisi.

35. The mystical writings of Bonaventure are collected in *Opuscula Mystica et Ad Ordinem Spectantia — Opera Omnia VIII* (Quaracchi, 1882 - 1911).

36. Reissued in *Tria Opuscula* (Quaracchi, 1964). All quotations are from the Quaracchi edition.

37. Etienne Delaruelle, "St. François D'Assise e La Pieté Populare," in *San Francesco nella ricerca* (Todi, 1971), p. 155.

38. In English: *The Little Flowers of St. Francis*, trans. Leo Sherley-Price (London, 1959); *The Little Flowers of St. Francis and Other Franciscan Writings*, trans. Serge Hughes (New York, 1964); *The Little Flowers of St. Francis*, trans. Raphael Brown (Garden City, 1958) reproduced with the

original introduction in *Omnibus*, pp. 1269 ff. I have translated the Francis stories in *Brother Francis* (New York, 1972).

39. Iris Origo, *The Merchant of Prato* (London, 1957).

40. The best Italian edition is *I Fioretti di San Francesco*, ed. Bughetti and Pratesi (Florence, 1959).

41. *Omnibus*, p. 888.

42. Edmund Gardner, "The Little Flowers of Saint Francis," in *Saint Francis of Assisi 1226 - 1926: Essays in Commemoration* (London, 1926), pp. 97 - 126.

43. Serge Hughes, *The Little Flowers*, p. 15.

44. Brown in *Omnibus*, p. 1286.

45. *Ibid.* An excellent bibliography on this subject begins on p. 1507.

46. Pompeati, *op. cit.*, p. 728.

47. Giovanni Getto, "Introduzione ai Fioretti," *Letteratura religiosa dal due al Novecento* (Firenze, 1967), p. 149.

48. *Chronica Fratris Jordani a Iano OFM. Analecta Franciscana I* (Quaracchi, 1885). This chronicle can be found in English in Placid Hermann, ed., *Thirteenth Century Chronicles* (Chicago, 1961), pp. 17 - 78. Hermann's edition is based on the French work by Marie-Therese Laureheilhe entitled *Sur Les Routes D'Europe au XIIIe Siècle* (Paris, 1959). All citations from the various chronicles are from Hermann's edition and simply cited as *Chronicles* in the footnotes.

49. The entire chronicle of Jordan was found by scholars imbedded in a much later chronicle written by a sixteenth century German friar named Nicholas Glassberger. This entire chronicle has been also published: *Chronica Fratris Nicolai Glassberger. Analecta Franciscana II* (Quaracchi, 1887).

50. Hermann in *Chronicles*, p. 16.

51. Published by Manchester University Press, 1951. There is an English edition: *The Coming of the Friars*, translated and introduced by L. Shirley-Price (London, 1964); also in *Chronicles*, pp. 91 - 192.

52. *Chronicles*, p. 87.

53. *Ibid.*, p. 161.

54. *Ibid.*, pp. 161 - 62.

55. The latest edition of this chronicle is *Salimbene di Adam: Cronica*, ed. Giuseppe Scalia, in 2 vol. (Bari, 1966); the older edition was *Cronica fratris Salimbene de Adam Ordinis Minorum*, ed. Oswald Holder-Egger (Hanover, 1905/13); *Chronicles*, pp. 217 - 90 has selections. There is not, to my knowledge, a complete version of Salimbene in English.

56. *Chronicles*, p. 202.

Chapter Four

1. *Oeuvres* X, p. 380, quoted in Omer Englebert, *Saint Francis: A Biography* (Chicago, 1965), pp. 24 - 25.

2. Hans Baron, "Franciscan Poverty and Civic Wealth As Factors in the Rise of Humanistic Thought," *Speculum* XIII (1938), pp. 1 - 37.

3. Quoted in Baron, p. 5.

4. Marvin Becker, "Lay Piety in Renaissance Florence," *The Pursuit of Holiness in Late Medieval and Renaissance Religion*, Charles Trinkaus and Heiko Oberman, eds. (Leiden, 1974), pp. 191 - 92.

5. Niccolo Machiavelli, *Opere*, edited by Mario Bonfantini (Milano, n.d.), p. 313.

6. Joseph Mazzeo, *Renaissance and Revolution* (London, 1967), pp. 109 - 10.

7. Englebert, cf. p. 25.

8. Wallace Ferguson, "The Reinterpretation of the Renaissance," in *Facets of the Renaissance* edited by William Werkmeister (New York: Harper Torchbook, 1963), pp. 1 - 18.

9. Ferguson, p. 10.

10. Matthew Arnold, "Pagan and Medieval Religious Sentiment," in *Lectures and Essays in Criticism* (1883) reprinted in *Complete Prose Works of Matthew Arnold* III (Ann Arbor, 1962), p. 224.

11. Quoted in Englebert, p. 32.

12. Sabatier's thesis has been best summarized by Sabatier himself in the introduction to his *Vie de St. François D'Assise* (Paris, 1894). I have retranslated that introduction and included it in my own anthology: *Brother Francis* (New York, 1972), pp. 22 - 31.

13. The International Congress of Franciscanists meeting in Assisi in 1973 devoted the whole of their congress to the theme of the "Franciscan Question from Sabatier to the Present"; the *Acta* of the congress were not available to the author.

14. *Saint Francis of Assisi: A Biography*, translated by T. O'Connor Sloane (London and New York, 1912) with many subsequent editions.

15. The entire question of the biographical tradition on Saint Francis after Sabatier has been studied by Raoul Manselli, in "I biografi moderni di San Francesco," *San Frescesco nella ricerae degli ultimi ottanta anni* (Todi, 1971), pp. 11 - 31.

16. Quoted in Emil Frederickson, "Giovanni Joergensen e L'Italia," *San Francesco: Patrone D'Italia* (February, 1967), p. 11. This monthly magazine from Assisi devoted that entire issue to various tributes to Joergensen who was considered one of the town's most illustrious citizens.

17. Nikos Kazantzakis, *Report to Greco* (New York, 1965), p. 378 ff.

18. Helen Kazantzakis, *Nikos Kazantzakis* (New York, 1969), p. 112; cf. also for a fuller study of this theme Lawrence S. Cunningham, "Saint Francis of Assisi and Nikos Kazantzakis," *The Cord* (June, 1974), pp. 31 - 36.

19. *Report to Greco*, p. 379.

20. *Ibid.*, p. 386.

21. On Simone Weil as a mystic in the age of the "death of God," see Susan Taubes "The Absent God," in *Towards a New Christianity: Readings*

in the Death of God Theology, edited by Thomas J. J. Altizer (New York, 1967), pp. 107 - 19; also Lawrence S. Cunningham, "Saint Francis of Assisi and Simone Weil," *The Cord* (February, 1974), pp. 53 - 58.

22. Simone Weil, *Waiting On God* (New York, 1951), p. 45.

23. *Ibid.*

24. I am indebted for my reading of this novel to the following critical works: Mark Boulby, *Hermann Hesse: His Mind and Art* (Ithaca, 1967); Ernest Rose, *Faith from the Abyss* (New York, 1957); *Peter Camenzind* may be found in the German original in *Gesammelte Schriften* I (Frankfort, 1957).

25. Gilbert K. Chesterton, "Saint Francis of Assisi," in *Simplicity and Tolstoy* (London, 1912).

26. Dudley Barker, *Gilbert Keith Chesterton* (New York, 1973), pp. 255 - 56.

27. Gilbert Keith Chesterton, *Saint Francis of Assisi* (London, 1923), p. 14. On the themes in Chesterton's own spirituality and their congeniality to Franciscan ideas, cf. Lawrence S. Cunningham, "Chesterton Reconsidered," *Thought* (Fall, 1972), pp. 271 - 79 and *idem*, "Chesterton as Mystic," *American Benedictine Review* (March 1975), pp. 16 - 24.

28. *Omnibus*, pp. 1699 - 1701.

29. That essay first appeared in *Science* (1967), pp. 1203 - 07; reprinted in *Brother Francis*, pp. 81 - 95.

30. Rene Dubos, "Franciscan Conservation versus Benedictine Stewardship," in *Ecology and Religion in History*, edited by David and Eileen Spring (New York: Harper Torchbook, 1974); this anthology also reproduces Lynn White's essay and other material pertinent to the topic.

31. Edward Armstrong, *Saint Francis: Nature Mystic* (Berkeley, 1973), p. 219.

32. Friedrich Heer, *The Medieval World* (New York, 1962), p. 224; Heer's *Intellectual History of Europe*, Volume I (New York, 1966), has also been very helpful and instructive in indicating the influence of Saint Francis on Western culture.

33. Heiko A. Oberman, "The Shape of Late Medieval Thought: the Birthpangs of the Modern Era," in *The Pursuit of Holiness in Late Medieval and Renaissance Religion*, eds. Charles Trinkaus and Heiko Oberman (Leiden, 1974), p. 7.

34. I denominate Ms. Erikson in this fashion not as a lapse into male chauvinism but because Erik Erikson was writing a book on Gandhi at the same time and was helped by his wife's work; Erikson wrote: "Her [Joan Erikson's] contemporaneous work on Saint Francis helped greatly to clarify the gay kind of sainthood also found in Gandhi," in *Gandhi's Truth* (New York, 1969), p. 14.

35. Joan Erikson, *Saint Francis and His Four Ladies.* (New York, 1970), p. 70.

36. Winston King, *Introduction to Religion: A Phenomenological Approach* (New York, 1968), p. 539 ff.

37. Michael Fisher, "Franciscan Community Life in the Anglican Church," *Centro Pro Unione* V (1973), pp. 27 - 28.

38. Freidrich Heiler, "Saint Francis of Assisi and the Catholic Church," *The Review of the Churches*, IV (1927), p. 328. I must thank Professor Paul Misner of Boston College for calling to my attention the interest of Heiler in things Franciscan.

Selected Bibliography

A bibliography of bibliographies is given in *A Francis of Assisi Research Bibliography*, compiled by Raphael Brown and printed as a supplement to Omer Englebert's *Saint Francis of Assisi* (Chicago: Franciscan Herald Press, 1965, pp. 508 - 09) and in *Saint Francis of Assisi: Omnibus of Sources* (Chicago: Franciscan Herald Press, 1972, pp. 1680 - 1681). *Bibliographia Franciscana* reviews current Franciscan scholarship and is published annually as a supplement to *Collectanea Franciscana* (Assisi and Rome, 1931 -).

PRIMARY SOURCES

Analecta Franciscana X. Quaracchi: Collegium Sanctae Bonaventurae, 1941. Contains (in Latin) Thomas of Celano's *First Life, Second Life, Legends for Choir Use, Treatise on the Miracles of Saint Francis;* Julian of Speyer's *Life of Saint Francis* and the *Rhymed Office;* Liturgical Offices, Sequences, and Masses in honor of Saint Francis; Elias of Cortona's *Encyclical Letter on the Death of Saint Francis;* the *Legenda Major and Legenda Minor* of Saint Bonaventure and *Lives of Saint Francis* (e.g., Jacques of Vitry's in the *Golden Legend*) adapted from the *Legendae* of Saint Bonaventure.

BONINO, GUIDO DAVICO, ed. *I fioretti di San Francisco.* Turin: Einaudi, 1968.

BUGHETTI, BENVENUTO, ed. *I fioretti di San Francisco.* Florence: Sansoni, 1959. Contains The *Little Flowers of Saint Francis; Considerations on the Stigmata;* the *Life of Brother Juniper;* the *Life and Sayings of Brother Egidius.* Good critical edition with important notes.

FAHY, BENEN, ed. *The Writings of Saint Francis of Assisi,* with notes by Placid Hermann. Chicago: Franciscan Herald Press, 1964. Reliable and scholarly.

HABIG, MARION, ed. *Saint Francis of Assisi: Writings and Early Biographies: English Omnibus of the Sources for the Life of Saint Francis.* Chicago: Franciscan Herald Press, 1973. Contains the writings of Saint Francis; the *Lives of Saint Francis* by Thomas of Celano; the *Lives of Saint Francis* by Saint Bonaventure; the *Legend of the Three Companions;* the *Legend of Perugia;* the *Mirror of Perfection;* the

143

Little Flowers of Saint Francis; the *Sacrum Commercium; Thirteenth Century Testimonies.* An excellent handbook of Franciscan studies with copious bibliographies and good introductions to each of the works given. Indispensable work in English.

HERMANN, PLACID, ed. and trans. *XIIIth Century Chronicles.* Chicago: Franciscan Herald Press, 1961. Contains the *Chronicle* of Jordan of Giano; the *Chronicle of the Coming of the Friars to England* by Thomas of Eccleston, and selections from the *Chronicle* of Friar Salimbene.

HUGHES, SERGE, trans. *The Little Flowers of Saint Francis and Other Franciscan Writings.* New York: Mentor Books, 1964. Good modern translation.

MANCINI, FRANCO, ed. *Jacopone da Todi: Laude. Scrittori d'Italia* no. 257. Bari: Laterza, 1975. Contains ninety-two lauds accepted by Mancini as authentic and six (including the *Stabat Mater)* as disputed. Important notes and glossary of terms. Indispensable.

Opuscula Sancti Patris Francisci Assisensis. 3rd ed. Quaracchi: Collegium Sanctae Bonaventurae, 1949. Contains all the Latin writings of the saint.

SECONDARY SOURCES

ARMSTRONG, EDWARD A. *Saint Francis: Nature Mystic. The Derivation and Significance of the Nature Stories in the Franciscan Legend.* Berkeley: University of California Press, 1973. Useful study especially for folklore motifs.

BARON, HANS. "Franciscan Poverty and Civic Wealth as Factors in the Rise of Humanistic Thought." *Speculum* III (1938), pp. 1 - 37. A fundamental study.

BRADY, IGNATIUS, ed. *The Marrow of the Gospel.* Chicago: Franciscan Herald Press, 1958. Essay translated from the German on the Franciscan Rule. Important studies.

BRANCA, VITTORE. "Il cantico di frate sole." *Archivium Franciscanum Historicum* XLI (1949), pp. 1 - 87. Important survey article with extensive bibliography.

BROOKE, ROSALIND. *Early Franciscan Government: From Elias to Bonaventure.* Cambridge: Cambridge University Press, 1959. Fundamental.

————. *Scripta Leonis, Ruffini et Angeli Sociorum.* Oxford: Clarendon Press, 1970. Important introduction.

CAMBELL, JACQUES. "Les Écrits de San François de Assise devant la Critique." *Franziskanische Studien* XXXVI (1954), pp. 82 - 109; 205 - 64. A basic study of the corpus of the writings of Saint Francis.

CHESTERTON, GILBERT. *Saint Francis of Assisi.* New York: Doubleday, 1924. Paperback edition, 1957. Eccentric but with brilliant insights into the life of the saint.

CUNNINGHAM, LAWRENCE, ed. *Brother Francis: Writings by and about Saint*

Francis of Assisi. New York: Harper and Row, 1972. Anthology of modern and ancient sources about the saint.

ENGLEBERT, OMER. *Saint Francis of Assisi.* Translated from the French by Eve Cooper. Chicago: Franciscan Herald Press, 1965. Appendices and bibliography especially important for historical study.

ESSER, CAJETAN. *The Origins of the Franciscan Order.* Chicago: Franciscan Herald Press, 1970. Fundamental historical study by outstanding Franciscan scholar.

FORTINI, ARNOLDO. *La Lauda in Assisi e le origini del teatro italiano.* Assisi: Città Nuova, 1961. A short polemical monograph.

_____. *Nova vita di san Francesco D'Assisi.* 5 vol. Assisi: Città Nuova, 1959. Vast study with many important documents. Indispensable.

GETTO, GIOVANNI. *Letterature religiosa dal due al novecenti,* Florence: Sansoni, 1967. Contains three important essays on Franciscan topics: a study of the *Canticle,* a study of the realism of Jacopone, and an essay on the *Fioretti.*

HEER, FREIDRICH. *The Medieval World.* New York: Mentor Books, 1962. Important reflections on Francis and his relationship to medieval culture.

Jacopone e il suo tempo. Convegni del centro di studi sulla spiritualità medievale. Todi: L'Accademia Tudertina, 1959. Important collection of essays and studies on Jacopone as poet, mystic, Franciscan.

JOERGENSEN, JOANNES. *Saint Francis of Assisi.* Translated from the Danish by T. O'Connor Sloane. New York and London: Longman Green & Co., 1912. Paperback edition, 1955. Dated but still useful; a Catholic response to Sabatier.

KAFTAL, GEORGE. *Saint Francis in Italian Painting.* Florence: Sansoni, 1955. Study of Franciscan iconography in late medieval and Renaissance painting.

LAMBERT, MALCOLM D. *Franciscan Poverty.* London: S.P.C.K., 1961. Important historical study. Fundamental.

MARINANGELI, B. "Le serie di affreschi giotteschi rappresentanti la vita di San Francesco." *Miscellanea Francescana* XII (1911), pp. 97 - 118. Study of the *titoli* under the Assisi frescos.

MEISS, MILLARD. *Giotto and Assisi.* New York: New York University Press, 1960.

_____, and TINTORI, LEONETTO. *The Painting of the Life of Saint Francis in Assisi.* New York: New York University Press, 1962. Technical study of the frescos.

MERTON, THOMAS. "Franciscan Eremitism." In *Contemplation in a World of Action,* pp. 273 - 81. Garden City: Image Books, 1973. Interesting study of a neglected area of Franciscan life.

MOORMAN, JOHN. *A History of the Franciscan Order.* Oxford: Oxford University Press, 1968. A scholarly survey of the life of Francis and the early Franciscans. Indispensable.

————. *Saint Francis of Assisi.* London: S.P.C.K., 1950. A nontechnical biography.

————. *Sources for the Life of Saint Francis of Assisi.* Manchester: University of Manchester Press, 1940. A fundamental study though now somewhat dated. Still valuable.

NESSI, SILVESTRO. "Jacopone da Todi al vaglio della critica moderna." *Miscellanea Francescana* LXIV (1964), pp. 404 - 32. A good survey of current scholarship on Jacopone.

————. "La vita di San Francesco depinta da Benozzo Gozzoli." *Miscellanea Francescana* LXI (1961), pp. 467 - 92. On the possible influence of the Spirituals on the Montefalco fresco cycle.

OZANAM, FREDERIC. *Les Poétes Franciscans en Italie au Triezieme Siècle.* Paris, 1852. Unreliable but important as part of the Romantic revival of Franciscan studies.

POMPEATI, ARTURO. *Letteratura Italiana: Il Medioevo.* Turin: U.T.E.T., 1965. Useful survey of the literary period at the time of Saint Francis.

RABY, F. J. E. *A History of Christian Latin Poetry.* Oxford: Oxford University Press, 1927. Has an informative and useful chapter on the Franciscan poets.

RAJA, P. "San Francesco e gli spiriti cavallereschi." *Nuova Antologia* (1926), pp. 387 - 99. Basic study of Saint Francis and Provençal culture.

SABATIER, PAUL. *Vie de Saint François d'Assise.* Paris: Fischbacher, 1893. English translation in 1894 and 1942. Dated and historically unreliable but still the single most influential biography of the saint.

San Francesco nella ricerca degli ultimi ottant'anni. Convegni del centro di studi sulla spiritualità medievale, IX. Todi: L'Accademi Tudertina, 1971. Important essays on Francis and biography; the *Canticle*, Francis, and Cardinal Hugolin, etc. Fundamental.

SMART, ALISTAIR. *The Assisi Problem and the Art of Giotto.* Oxford: Oxford University Press, 1971. Crucial study with a vast bibliography.

SMITH, JOHN H. *Saint Francis of Assisi.* New York: Scribners, 1972. Paperback edition, 1975. Francis from a Jungian perspective. Erratic but useful.

THODE, HENRY. *Franz von Assisi und die Anfänge der Kunst der Renaissance in Italien.* Berlin, 1885. Pioneering work that linked Franciscanism to the emerging period of the Renaissance.

VAN CORSTANJE, A. *The Covenant with God's Poor: An Essay on the Biblical Interpretation of the Testament of Saint Francis of Assisi.* Chicago: Franciscan Herald Press, 1966. Good bibliography on Franciscan spirituality.

VAN DIJK, S., and WALKER, J. *The Origins of the Modern Roman Liturgy: The Liturgy of the Roman Court and the Franciscan Order in the Thirteenth Century.* Westminster: Newman Press, 1960. A fundamental study.

WHITE, LYNN. "The Historical Roots of Our Ecological Crisis." *Science* (1967), pp. 1203 - 7. Often anthologized. A provocative study of Saint Francis on nature and his relationship to our culture.

ADDENDUM

After completion of this manuscript there appeared two extremely important books that bear on the subject of this study. E. Randolph Daniel's *The Franciscan Concept of Mission in the High Middle Ages* (Lexington: University of Kentucky, 1975) is an attempt to argue against the Sabatier thesis by a refocus of the question so as not to make the question of poverty a central one. David Jeffrey's *The Early English Lyric and Franciscan Spirituality* (Lincoln: University of Nebraska, 1975) argues that fully 90% of early English lyrics were written under the influence of models coming from Franciscan preaching, song, and poetry.

Index

Actus Beati Francisci, 98 - 99
Ageno, Franca, 70
Agnello, Brother, 38
Agnes of Prague, Blessed, 22
Angela of Foligno, Blessed, 41
Anglican Franciscans, 126 - 27
Anthony of Padua, Saint, 37, 41, 79, 99
Armstrong, Edward: *Saint Francis: Nature Mystic,* 123 - 24
Arnold, Matthew, 113 - 14
Arbor Vitae Crucifixae, see Ubertino da Casale

Bardi Chapel, 85
Baron, Hans, 109 - 110
Bartholomew of Pisa: *De Conformitate Vitae Sancti Francisci,* 85
Becker, Marvin, 110 - 11
Benedict of Arezzo, 87
Bernardino of Siena, Saint, 41
Boniface VIII, Pope, 68, 69, 72
Bonaventure, Saint, 21, 25, 41, 74 - 75, 76, 100; *Itinerarium Mentis Ad Deum,* 25, 67, 75, 97 - 98; *Legenda Major,* 59, 81, 93 - 98; *Legenda Minor,* 95
Bonizo of Bologna, 18
Brady, Ignatius, 122
Brooke, Rosalind, 91 - 92
Brown, Raphael, 101
Burckhardt, Jacob, 112 - 13, 115

Caesar of Speyer, 17
Cambell, Jacques, 26, 38
Capuchins, The, 109
Catani, Peter, 17
Celestine V, Pope, 68, 72
Chesterton, Gilbert Keith, 55, 120 - 21

Cimabue, 74 - 75
Clare of Assisi, Saint, 15, 16, 22, 31, 51
Colonna Family, The, 68, 69
Compilatio Perusina, 30
Continuatio Saxonica, 103
Crescentius of Jesi, 79, 88
Cuthbert of Brighton, Father: *Life of Saint Francis,* 121 - 22

Dante, 14, 66, 69, 81, 95, 110, 111
Day, Dorothy, 126
Declaration of Longhezza, The, 68
Delaruelle, Eugene, 98
DeSanctis, Francesco, 75
Dies Irae, see Thomas of Celano
Dionysius the Areopagite, see Pseudo Dionysius
Duns Scotus, John, 41
Dubos, Rene, 122

Eckhart, Meister, 40
Elias of Cortona, Brother, 36, 83, 87, 100, 102, 103
Englebert, Omer, 112, 122
Erigena, John Scotus, 55, 76
Erikson, Joan: *Saint Francis and His Four Ladies,* 124
Esser Cajetan, 24, 27, 37, 51

Ferguson, Wallace, 113
Fioretti, The, 25, 95, 98 - 102, 109, 116
Five Considerations on the Stigmata, 99
Frugoni, Arsenio, 71
Francis of Assisi, Saint, (1181? - 1226): early descriptions of, 86; mysticism, 39 - 40; significance of prose work, 38 - 41; poetic influence of, 59 - 67;

modern interpretations of, 109 - 26; Stigmata of, 23, 86, 97, 105
WRITINGS: POETRY:
"Canticle of Brother Sun," 13 - 14, 44, 46, 47, 51 - 59, 84
Office of the Passion, 49 - 51
"Praises before the Office," 48 - 49
"Praises of the Most High," 42 - 45
"Praises of the Virtues," 45 - 47
"Salutation to the Virgin," 47 - 48
WRITINGS: PROSE:
Admonitions, The, 25 - 27, 44
Disputed Prose Works, 36 - 38
Letters, 31 - 36
Rules for Hermitages, 23 - 25
Rules of Life, 15 - 23
Testaments, The, 27 - 31
Franciscan Chronicles, see Jordan of Giano, Salimbene, Thomas Eccleston
Franciscan Orders, 126 - 28

Garzo, 63
Getto, Giovanni, 56, 101
Giacomino da Verona: *Heavenly Jerusalem and Infernal Babylon*, 64 - 66
Gibbon, Edward, 12
Giotto, 14, 82, 89, 95 - 97
Goethe, 109, 129
Gozzoli, Benozzo, 97
Greccio, 84, 85, 87
Gregory IX, Pope, 22, 79, 83, 96, 103
Guido da Montefeltro, 69

Hardick, Lothar, 38
Heer, Friedrich, 22, 123
Heiler, Friedrich, 128 - 29
Henry of Avanches: *Legenda Versificata*, 87
Hermann, Placid, 79, 84, 104, 105, 108
Hesse Hermann: *Peter Camenzkind*, 119 - 20
Honorius III, Pope, 18
Hughes, Serge, 99, 100
Hugolin, see Gregory IX
Hutton, Edward, 60

Illuminato, Fra, 94
Innocent III, Pope, 15
Italian Biographers of Francis, 122

Jacopo da Massa, 99
Jacopa da Settesoli, 36, 37
Jacopone da Todi, 42, 62, 67 - 76
Jeffries, Richard, 54
Joachim of Flora, 21, 63, 71
Joergensen, Johannes: *Saint Francis of Assisi*, 115 - 17
John of Celano, 87
John of the Cross, 40, 71
John of Fidanza, see Bonaventure, Saint
John of Parma, 78, 88, 91
Jordan of Giano: *Chronicle*, 102 - 104
Julian of Speyer: *Vita Sancti Francisci*, 87

Kazantzakis, Nikos: *Francis of Assisi*, 117 - 18
King, Winston, 125

Latini, Brunetto, 110
Laudario Cortonese, 63
laudesi, The movement of the, 62 - 64
Legend of Perugia, 93
Legend of the Three Companions, The, 25, 37, 60, 81, 91 - 93
Legenda Versificata, see Henry of Avanches
Legendae of Thomas of Celano, see Thomas of Celano
Lemmens, Leonard, 116
Leo, Brother, 18, 31 - 32, 42 - 43, 72, 93, 99
Little, A. G., 104
Little Flowers of Saint Francis, The, see *Fioretti*

Machiavelli, Niccolo, 110
Mancini, Franco, 70
Master of Saint Francis Cycle, The, 96
Mazzeo, Joseph, 112
Merton, Thomas, 24
Moorman, Joseph, 16, 20, 32, 92, 95, 104
Mystic Marriage of Saint Francis and Lady Poverty, 82

Origen, 40
Origo, Iris: *The Merchant of Prato*, 98
Ozanam, Frederick, 76, 78, 112

Parenti, Giovanni, 37, 79
Peacham, John: *Philomena*, 66 - 67
Petrarch, 63, 110
Pompeati, Arturo, 63, 101
Pseudo-Dionysius, 39, 71, 76

Quo Elongati, 29

Ramakrishna, 125
Renan, Ernest, 114, 128
Ruskin, John, 41

Sabatier, Paul, 18, 19, 20, 29, 30, 37, 38, 81, 92, 98, 113, 114 - 15, 129
Sacrum Commercium, 78 - 83
Salimbene, Fra: *Chronicle*, 106 - 108
Salmi, Mario, 74
San Damiano, church of, 15, 33
Santa Croce, church of, 89
Schweitzer, Albert, 118
Simon of Ashby, 104
Smart, Alastair, 96 - 97
Speculum Majus, 30
Speculum Perfectionis, 39, 53, 92 - 93
Stabat Mater, 61, 70, 75, 135n
Subiaco, 86

Teresa of Calcutta, Mother, 126
Thode, Henry, 78, 112

Thomas of Celano, 13, 43, 51, 53; *Ad Usum Chori*, 87; *Dies Irae*, 61; *First Life (Legenda Prima)*, 79, 80, 83 - 86; *Second Life (Legenda Secunda)*, 45, 60, 87 - 93; *Tractatus de Miraculis*, 91
Thomas of Eccleston: *Chronicle*, 105 - 106
Thomas of Muntzer, 22

Ubertino da Casale: *Arbor Vitae Crucifixae*, 34, 81, 83
Ugolino da Boniscambi, 99
Ugolino da Brunforte, 98 - 99
Umbrian Dialect, 52
Underhill, Evelyn, 72

Victorine mystics, 76
Voltaire, 109

Wadding, Luke, 15, 51
Waldo, Peter, 22
Watson, Paul Rev., 127
Weil, Simone, 118 - 19
White, Lynn, 55, 122 - 23
White, Mother Lurana, 127
Wordsworth, William, 41, 54